Milestones
for **Global Leaders'** **Success** in the United States

First published in the Republic of Korea in February, 2025 MAOWR Inc.

Copyright © 2025 by Evan Eun Sung Kim
All rights reserved. No part of this book may be reproduced, stored in a retrieval system, or transmitted in any form or by any means, electronic, mechanical, photocopying, recording, scanning, or otherwise without permission of the author and publisher.

Inquiries should be addressed to
MAOWR Inc.
1 Seohyeon-ro 210beon-gil, #405
Bundang-gu, Seongnam-si 13591
Gyeonggi-do, South Korea
Tel: +82-31-8028-0202
Email: business@maowr.com
Website: www.maowr.com

ISBN 979 11 983891 3 8   03320

Milestones
for Global Leaders' Success
in the United States

Evan Eun Sung Kim

Contents

Prologue   Global Business Leader • 8

Foreword
A Message of Advice for Global Leaders

Hidden Leader
   Who Shows the Path to Becoming a Global Leader • 14
By Song, Young Soo

The "Initial Power" of Thriving in a Multicultural Organization • 16
By Eom, Jun Ha

Mind's Compass on a Phenomenal Journey •18
By James Roh

A Guide to Understand American Society and Organizations • 20
By James Roh

I. American Society
Respect, Honesty, Trust, Attention and Care, Family-Like

Organizing • 24

Marathon • 31

The Vision of the Company and Me • 37

Gossip • 45

Compensation and Motivation • 52

Diversity and Inclusion • 59

Communication and Listening • 65

Efficiency and Effectiveness • 76

Good Company • 89

From "Myself" to "We" and "Together" • 95

Work Life and Satisfaction • 102

Five Core Values for Communication and Relationships • 108

Why Eat Together? • 114

II. American Organization
"STAND" Makes Leader 101 a Reality

Personal Management Innovation • 122

My Between Words and Actions • 129

Diagnostic Technique for Leaders • 136

The Age of Lifelong Learning • 144

The Difference Between a Pro and an Amateur • 151

Harmonization of the Viewpoint • 158

Change for Improvement and Growth
   Is Not an Option but Mandatory • 165

The Distance Between Colleagues • 172

An Attitude of a Leader with Dignity • 178

The Lubricant of Relationships • 185

The Give-and-Take Formula • 191

Basics • 198

The Class of Leaders
   Who Will Set Nations and Organizations Right • 203

A Truly Professional Manager • 209

The Necessity of Non-Business
   Communication and Relationships • 215

III. American Business
Understand Melting Pot and Salad Bowl First

Individualism and Collectivism Coexist • 224

Cultural Generalization Boundaries • 230

A Gap Between Formal and Pragmatic Logic • 235

Sharing the Korean Sentiment • 242

Stereotypes and Misconceptions About the United States • 248

The Difference Between Friendliness and Friendship • 254

Inherent Characteristics of United States Organizations • 261

Basic Manners in American Organizations • 274

Epilogue
Competencies Required
   for Leading Diverse Organizations in the United States • 282

Prologue

Global Business Leader

Writing this prologue has been one of the most challenging aspects of preparing this book. Reflecting on the book's clear purpose, key points, and the meaningful message that I wish to convey to readers has reminded me of the responsibility and pressure that come with sharing a lifetime of experience and insights.

I began my career as an engineer at a major Korean company in 1981. Four years later, I was transferred to the United States as an expatriate. Over the next 40 years, I took on various roles, including managing business projects, sales, HR development, organizational dynamics, and management consulting for both Korean and American companies. I also established my own management consulting firm, specializing in the intersection of Korean and American business practices.

Through these diverse experiences, I developed expertise in Korean-American culture and global organizational management. Now, I feel compelled to share these insights with executives and employees of multinational corporations in Korea, Korean-American companies in the U.S., and American companies. As multinational organizations continue to expand in today's globalized world, I hope the lessons I've learned over more than 40 years in the U.S. will provide valuable advice and guidance to readers.

So far, I have published four books on American culture and business practices. While I am not a scholar or a professor and do not rely on theories, laws, or academic frameworks, my 40 years of hands-on experience-interacting with people and navigating various roles as an executive, manager, and educator-have taught me valuable lessons about the differences between Korean and American business practices and cultures, as well as the reasons behind them.

One of the most important insights I have gained is the need to unify individuals with diverse mindsets and cultural backgrounds to work toward a shared goal.

To achieve this, I immersed myself in American corporate life, observing how problems are solved, results are achieved, and relationships are built. I focused on respecting diversity within the organizations while fostering unity among employees. Over time, I developed programs, systems, campaigns, and training methods tailored to these organizations' specific needs, proving effective in both the short and long term.

This book is structured into three main chapters, each reflecting my personal experiences and insights.

Chapter 1 explores the environment and characteristics of Korean companies operating in the U.S. and, purely American companies. It provides practical strategies for maximizing productivity and achieving results in global organizations across diverse cultures. Chapter 2 focuses on essential management techniques, communication strategies, and relationship-building methods for successful leadership in multicultural organizations. Drawing from hands-on, practical experience, this chapter offers key insights into organizational behavior that integrate Korean and American business perspectives. Chapter 3 delves into American culture and business practices. Understanding Americans, their culture, and their business norms is crucial for fostering effective organizational relationships and collaboration. Even with excellent products, services, and systems, cultural misunderstandings can undermine trust and hinder teamwork. This chapter updates examples from my earlier books, "The Guide to Living in America" and "Why do Koreans wear white socks with formal suits?" to reflect current trend and insights.

This book is written primarily for several key audiences: Korean expatriates and their families working for Korean companies in the U.S.; Korean immigrants to the U.S.; first- and second-generation Koreans and Americans aspiring to work for global or multicultural companies; and Korean entrepreneurs seeking insights into U.S. business practices.

Additionally, I hope to connect with managers navigating similar stages in their professional and personal lives. I trust this book will provide valuable and meaningful insights, helping readers achieve their societal, organizational and personal goals.

As I compiled the topics and stories that shaped my 40 years in the U.S., I felt deep gratitude for the many organizations, friends and colleagues in both Korea and the U.S., who have contributed to this journey.

I would like to express my heartfelt gratitude to Mr. Yongjin Chang, Chairman of Kiss Products, for his generous support; Professor Young Soo Song of Hanyang University for his invaluable advice; and MAOWR, a talent creation company, for their diligent editing and supervision.

Lastly, I dedicate this book to my wife and two daughters, whose unwavering belief in me has been a constant source of encouragement throughout my life, and to my parents, who, even in their 90s, continue to love and support me unconditionally.

Evan Eun Sung Kim

Foreword
A Message of Advice for Global Leaders

Hidden Leader
Who Shows the Path to Becoming a Global Leader

By Song, Young Soo

The phrase "Hidden Champion" was coined by renowned German business scholar Hermann Simon to describe global blue-chip companies excelling in their respective fields. Just as there are hidden champions among companies, there are also "hidden leaders" who drive growth, shaping the future of these global firms while creating a legacy of challenges and pioneering success.

While famous executives like Steve Jobs of Apple and Bill Gates of Microsoft are well known, the competitive advantage of global blue-chip companies often stems from the effort of leaders working behind the scenes. These hidden leaders lay the foundation for sustainable growth, turning ideas into reality and achieving extraordinary results.

From this perspective, the author of this book stands as an undisputed hidden leader. His story of over 40 years of passion and dedication in corporate America reveals not just how to survive, but how to thrive and succeed as leader in American society and organizations during the era of the Fourth Industrial

Revolution and Digital Transformation.

Most notably, the author is a seasoned expatriate management veteran, having lived and breathed expatriate life. If you are an expatriate, or aspiring to become one, an executive, an HR professional, a regional expert, or a young leader seeking to do business globally—especially in the U.S.—this book offers invaluable insights.

This book is not intended to cover every aspect of American society or business. Rather, it is a candid, experience-driven account of the author's life in the corporate world of the U.S. The phrase "HIS + STORY = HISTORY" makes this story both compelling and thought-provoking.

As the saying goes, "reading is a sitting-down journey." For readers looking to succeed in America and corporate America, this book serves as a powerful starting point on that seated journey.

Song, Young Soo

Prof. Song has spent 23 years as an expert in leadership and human resource development at Samsung and has been a professor of education at Hanyang University since 2006, dedicated to fostering the growth of his students. He has served as director of the Leadership Center, the Happiness Dream Counseling Center, and the Human Resource Development Center at Hanyang University. As one of Korea's leading experts in talent development, Professor Song has also held prestigious roles as the president of the Korean Academy of Leadership and the Korean Society for Human Resource Development.

The "Initial Power" of Thriving in a Multicultural Organization

By Eom, Jun Ha

Life is a series of challenges. These challenges are even more frequent when you choose a particular path, and how you respond to each one can define your success or failure. That is why having a plan at every stage of life is crucial-without one, you're drifting without direction.

This book provides the foundation for such a plan. The author draws on 40 years of lived experience to offer insights into understanding and adapting to American society and organizations. It highlights not only the importance of skills but also the significant of the right posture, attitude, and values when engaging with American society and organizations. In fact, a person's attitude is often more impactful than their abilities or efforts. No matter how competent or hardworking you are, if your attitude is misaligned, it can have negative consequences for both society and your organization.

This book offers readers the "Initial Power" to succeed in American society and organizations. The word "Initial" comes from the Latin word meaning "beginning" and initial power refers to strength to spark change. In other words, this book provides the motivation and willpower to establish yourself in American society and thrive in organizational settings.

Initial power frequently leads to self-directed learning, where individuals take responsibility for their own growth by tailoring their learning style to their personal interests and needs. This enhanced motivation and effectiveness, combining existing knowledge with new experiences to develop greater competencies. Such self-directed learning is critical for anyone aspiring to lead in a multicultural organization in the United States.

An American psychologist William James once said, "Change your thoughts, and you change your behavior; change your behavior and your habits; change your habits and your character; change your character and you change your destiny." This book aims to help readers refine their thinking, put that thinking into action, and build habits that will prepare them step up as leaders in multicultural organizations.

Eom, Jun Ha

Chairman Eom holds a PhD in human resource development and has spent over 30 years studying how to develop and unleash the innate talents of individuals. He is a pioneer in the field of HRD, committed to fostering people's capabilities within organizations and advancing the ideas of "people-centered management" and "a world of humanity" through HRD. He is currently the chairman of the Korea Human Resource Development Association, principal of Life Management School, and publisher of Monthly HRD.

Mind's Compass on a Phenomenal Journey

By James Roh

Living in a foreign country is never easy. Whether you are an entrepreneur, expatriate, or employee, working abroad requires significant preparation to navigate the complexities of language, dialect, values, mindset, history and culture.

Among these, mental preparation stands out as the most important. If I were to describe Tripitaka Koreana in one word, it would be "mindfulness." This concept is central to the uniqueness of this book. The author, who has been active in American society and organizations for over 40 years, shares his knowledge and experience, relentlessly exploring the mindset required to succeed as a leader in unfamiliar environments.

He demonstrates how vision, mission, and core values are projected into one's life and, in turn, shape that life. This life, when properly directed, is filled with happiness, growth, and a sense of wonder. The author stresses that execution is the key to realizing these goals and offers wisdom on managing negative and consuming emotions that often arise in the mind.

If you look closely, our lives are built on a foundation of

spontaneity. Those who understand this principle can ignite their passion in every moment, achieve joyful and surprising outcomes, and enrich their lives. The author infuses his own experiences of living as a spontaneous individual into this book, and his life of conviction and unity of action serves as inspiration to those who merely dream without action.

The path to leadership in American society—especially in a multicultural organization—is challenging. There are no ready-made answers; there is only your own "phenomenal journey" that await beyond your current self. This book acts as a compass to help you navigate that personal journey.

In support of everyone who dreams of a successful journey in American society and multicultural organizations, the author shares a verse from the "Sutta Nipata," that holds deep meaning for him.

Go alone like a lion that is not startled by loud noises, like the wind that does not get caught in a net, like a lotus that does not get wet by water, and like the horn of a rhinoceros that walks alone in the wilderness.

James Roh

Chairman Roh holds an MBA from Whitworth University and a PhD in Psychology from Sungkyunkwan University. He has worked at Samsung Electronics and currently serves as the Chairman of the Board of Carrot Global. In this role, he plays a pivotal part in nurturing the next generation of talent through expatriate training, global job competency education, and leadership consciousness-advancement training.

A Guide to Understand American Society and Organizations

By Kim, Young Hun

A book that is truly essential for the global era has arrived. In this work, the author draws on 40 years of experience in American society and organizations—gained through establishing and managing Korean companies in the U.S., working with American businesses, and leading management consulting firms.

This is not a book of theory, but one based on real-life trial and error, making it a practical guide for those involved in multicultural organizations. It will also be highly valuable for executives preparing to enter the U.S. market and for business coaches advising them on navigating this complex environment.

The author highlights communication and listening as the most crucial elements for success in multicultural organizations in the United States. By recognizing the cultural differences that can lead to mistakes and misunderstandings, readers will be better equipped to avoid these common pitfalls. Additionally, the book emphasizes five core values essential for interpersonal relationships in organizations: respect, honesty, trust, integrity, and family. It offers practical advice on how to apply these values effectively.

The author also explores how to transition from being an amateur to a professional in a multicultural organization. The key lies in staying grounded and committing to lifelong learning. This helps overcome pride and prejudice, ultimately shaping individuals into true leaders.

The importance of action is a central theme, echoing Einstein's sentiment that "nothing changes until it moves." In multicultural organizations, the challenges and trials are constant, but by internalizing the necessary knowledge and experience through practice, one can navigate these environments smoothly and effectively.

I strongly recommend keeping this book close as a guide to acquiring the knowledge, skills, and attitudes necessary for adapting to and leading in a multicultural American organization.

Kim, Young Hun

Chairman Kim has worked at POSCO for over 30 years in key roles in human resources development and innovation. He has held positions such as head of the HR team, secretary general, head of the management support division at POSCO Chemicals, president of the POSCO Academy of Future Planning, and vice president of administration at POSTEK. Recently, he served as the president of the Korea Coach Association. Currently, he is a professor of coaching science at KyungHee University Business School and a columnist for Hankyung.COM.

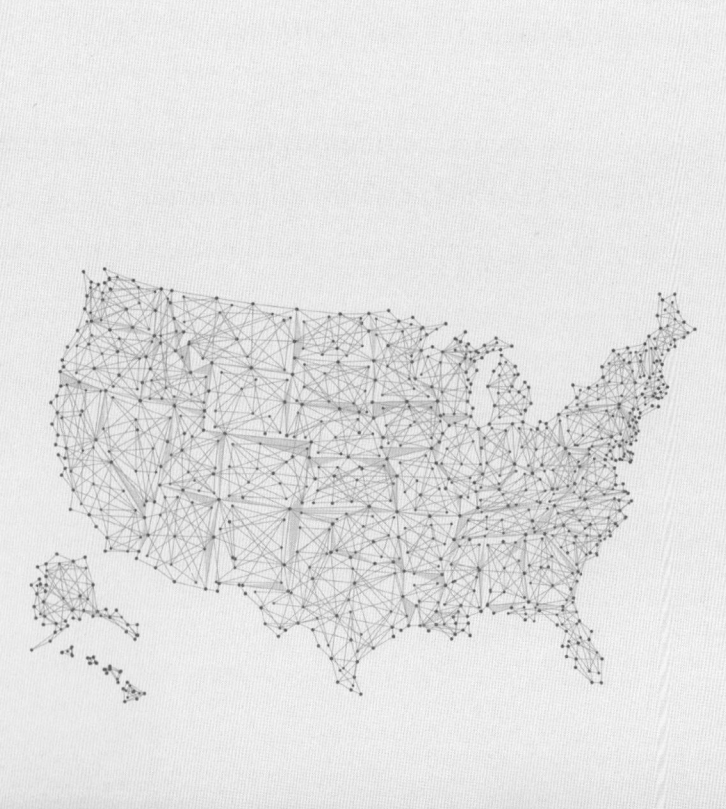

I

American Society

For Your Social and Organizational life,

Show **Respect** and **Honesty**

Then, Earn **Trust**

With **Attention** and **Care**,

We Become **Family-Like**

Organizing

Discard unnecessities

You probably have seen an office scene in movies where a man frantically picks up a business call amidst piles of papers and files on the desk. These scenes give us the illusion that people are working so hard. However, if we look closer, we need to think about whether a cluttered working environment is good enough for managing tasks efficiently and effectively.

Some groups in the organization are multi-taskers, able to handle multiple things simultaneously. In contrast, another group of people are single-taskers, focusing on one thing at a time. Nevertheless, before we talk about how work gets done, we should consider the working environment; and organizing is closely associated with it.

Once or twice a year, I used to send an official memo to the organization where I belong requesting to tie up their desks and surroundings. The idea of regular notice of something as common sense as this may surprise managers highly experienced, but its importance cannot be underestimated.

A phrase in the "Nidec Corporation History" book says, that among the basic attitudes and habits of company life is to be modest, neat, polite, organized, tidy, and clean. This message sounds too obvious, however, the message behind it is that by sticking to the basics, you will be able to handle tough tasks and difficult relationships.

There was once a TV show craze in the US about compulsive hoarding syndrome, a condition in which people obsess over things. The show was about people who could not get rid of stuff such as electronics, furniture, clothing, and all sorts of things they owned. At some point, they became unmanageable, buried themselves in their stuff, and could not live normally. They may have started collecting one thing after another with the best intentions, frugality, and fulfilling sentimental value. But in the end, they are stuck in a lonely, miserable life, unable to control their lives or even interact with people, instead of dependent on the things they choose.

Every spring or autumn in the United States, tons of electronics, furniture, and stuff are piled up on a curbside around residents. These discards during the cleaning season are picked up by the town's sanitation department on a set date. It is not a surprise that unexpected items are explored throughout

Organized desk.

the seasonal cleaning process that were forgotten in the memory. Obviously, the items would have been bought for their purpose. However, its value and meaning have changed over time within their thought and the environment. Eventually, most of those items became junk. As such, we continue to produce material, mental, and emotional garbage in our lives, and some of us are paranoid about throwing it away.

We also have similar experiences at work. We utilize information, materials, and suppliers, including files and papers, when performing tasks. The longer your career, the greater the variety and quantity. While organizing, you are likely to find a lot of information and things piled up even though you have not looked for them in a while or do not need them.

I remember my 30s with stacks of papers on the desk. I meant to evoke the image of someone busy in an office like in a movie, but perhaps I was meant to show American coworkers that I work so hard and busy.

Though decades later, my seat and surroundings are much tidier and cleaner than anyone in the organization. One of the things I've learned over my career and life experiences is that organizing is one of the key elements to success. I can maximize the efficiency of my work and time management when I prioritize organizing. Being organized, not only in the surroundings but also in the information to work with, as well as in my mind and attitude, allowed me to execute tasks and plans in a more rational and organized manner.

I have also found reaching the goal and accomplishing the result much faster when working on this process. Having the knowledge and information required to do my job organized around me and in my head allowed me to prioritize what I needed to do and how to approach each task so I could effectively and efficiently spend my time and effort to achieve my goals.

Organizing reduces unnecessary and repetitive work, irrational communication, unexpected errors, and omissions, and achieving optimal productivity with the least time and effort. Not surprisingly, individual confidence and organizational performance are bound to increase.

Moreover, you can focus on your work with more time even in your daily life if you are organized. You can also change your defensive work habits, where you are passive amid busyness, frenzy, and anxiety.

Being organized is a process of knowing and sorting out what you should do or not, and the priority of important and unnecessary things. Additionally, it is about placing necessary resources and tools in the right place.

When you are organized, you can see your priorities clearly, so you can work efficiently and get things done effectively. Eventually, being organized is a realistic, practical, and common-sense preparation for getting things done.

I used certain terms to talk about physical and mental organizing to my co-workers: "prioritization," "80:20 rule," and "ABCD rule." These terms are generalized concepts from a business aspect and are recommended to use since they are highly beneficial ways to stay organized at work.

First, "prioritization" is listing the key things you plan to do under headings and then arranging them in order of importance and necessity.

> The "80:20 rule" has the meaning
> of accomplishing 80 percent of your final goal
> if you perform in the top 20 percent among the entire list.

Then apply the "80:20 rule" to the entire prioritized list. The "80:20 rule" has the meaning of accomplishing 80 percent of your final goal if you perform in the top 20 percent among the entire list. Thus, you can achieve more than the rest of the 80 percent if you perform the top 20 percent properly. This proves to have completely different outcomes with the same amount of time and effort if you do things based on importance and necessity.

The "ABCD rule" is to classify your tasks with "ABCD." Category A is a "must-do" and mandatory tasks, and category B is not as important as A but requires responsibility. Category C requires an execution, but something that lower-level employees can handle. Thus, you can focus on categories A and B while delegating category C tasks based on your value and capacity. Meanwhile, category D is an unnecessary task that should ultimately be eliminated. These are tasks done out of habit, overlooked, or ignored, without applying critical thinking.

The outcomes of organizing would get better when you apply these three rules as a guiding principle.

We shouldn't just be doing the physical organizing, but the metaphysical organizing as well; if we are organizing our physical environment, we should also be organizing our mental state.

We accumulate a lot of negative emotions in our daily lives and work for various reasons, such as worry, anxiety, frustration, dissatisfaction, anger, excuses, greed, impatience, and other mental garbage that make our minds sick. If we clean out this mental garbage and fill it with positive emotions like dreams, hopes, determination, passion, purity, caring, humility, and love, our work and lives will be more abundant.

I am reminded of the Ven. Beop Jeong, talk about non-possession. His emphasis on non-possession does not mean possessing nothing, but not possessing anything unnecessary. As a lifelong practitioner of non-possession and the fulfillment of emptiness, this kind of mind organization would have kept him in tip-top shape, allowing him to engage in his practice fully.

From that perspective, I also try to keep myself tense and continue to be organized in daily life.

Marathon

I hate running!

I've worked at several companies in the U.S., and one of them had a training center located in the Pocono resort area, Pennsylvania. The training course I led then was a multi-day camp training program, including promotional training, position-specific training, newcomer training, leadership training, functional enhancement workshop, etc. While the content varied depending on the program, there was a common schedule, morning jogs.

We gathered in front of the training center around 7:00 in the morning to prepare for jogging no matter what season it was. Every time I went for a jog, I heard a voice of complaint, saying, "It's too cold," "It's too hot," "It's about to rain," "My body hurts," "I'm tired from last night's event," "I'm exhausted," etc.

Especially in the winter, trainees feel even more particularly piteous. Most of them are dressed in thick outerwear, hunkered down in the cold, with their hands in their pockets. Some were almost half asleep with their eyelids drooping, and some were pouting their lips, and sometimes you would find a few resentful glares.

Moreover, some of them requested payment for overtime via formal email at the end of the course that the morning jogs are performed outside of training requested by the company, so it should be paid. A similar case has occurred recently in Korea, but it was a common occurrence in the United States for a long time.

In this atmospheric pressure, we warm up safely and then start chanting and jogging. Normally we take around 2.5 miles in 40 minutes which is not a severe running condition.

After the jog, we shower and eat breakfast, and then the morning schedule begins. I give the first lecture of the course on the topic "A Marathon is a Microcosm of Life," which is related to the morning jog.

Some of the trainees complained that because the instructor liked morning jogs, was good at them, wanted to show off, or wanted to reign over. However, they all changed to positive attitudes via this lecture. The contents of the lecture are as follows:

> Everyone, running a marathon or jogging is a lot like our lives. No one can run for you, and only you can for yourself.

Jogging is for anyone who is willing to do it and has at least physical strength. So, I encourage you to look at your condition and current level. As you know, a marathon only ends when you reach your destination. No matter how fast you are, if you do not reach the final destination, you are not done.

Even as a jogger by nature, when I start running, I have all sorts of reasons to stop running in mind. It's too cold or too hot, I need a break, I'm sore, I'm out of breath, etc. Every day is different, and your physical and mental condition vary.

However, everyone who exercises regularly experiences and acknowledges that after some time, habits are developed to support both mind and body, without psychological complaints and physical strain. You will no longer experience any strife while exercising once you reach this level. Your mind gets relaxed and so does your

Go for it!

breathing, and your body unconsciously moves with inertia. The consistent exercises you have been reluctant to do, including jogging, allow your physical capacity enhancement. Through the repetition of this process, at some point, you will reach a state of spontaneous engagement.

This process of internalizing exercise can apply to various situations in life. You can learn a "just do it" attitude, where you don't use circumstances or conditions as an excuse for not executing your goals or plans, don't give up, and just try.

Like a marathon, running alone might be lonely, but it also helps to realize the way of the world. You will learn that life does not always go your way while you deal with cold, hot, and many other challenges.

By the time you reach the finish line, salted sweat feels sweet, scorching soles become warm, and heavy muscles are relaxed and comfortable. When I take a deep breath and look up, the blue sky even looks more beautiful, and so do our lives.

The morning jog aims to share these lessons with you, and I hope you can take this experience and apply it to your work and daily life to make your life more positive.

My morning routine before work is going to the gym and work out for an hour. I stretch, run, and lift weights, but no intention or desire to get a six-pack. I just do it to keep a healthy mind and body to contribute to my family and society. I agree with the phrase "My body is my asset," especially as I get older. No matter how smart you are, how high up you are, how wealthy you are, if you lose your health, you can't do anything about it. And your body becomes your liability.

People are usually good at drawing up and sticking to a new plan like exercising, but they are also good at dropping out for one reason or another. It is not easy to keep doing without a clear purpose or a firm commitment to your goal. Once you have had the experience of starting and finishing something at least once, you will have a much easier time achieving your goals the next time. If you gradually get used to the experience of achievement, make it a habit so that it becomes a subconscious process.

I found that people who take action on their life goals usually speak in the present tense, whereas those who are not are more likely to use past, future, or anticipatory tenses as excuses. For example, "So I couldn't do it," "I am going to do it," or "I should do it." However, people who are practicing their life goals do not give excuses. Because they are "now," "just," and "doing" it.

Speed, distance, and time are the main evaluation factors when we attempt our goals. People applaud the value of faster, further, and longer. But people are most impressed with an attitude of accomplishing without giving up until the end through will, passion, and sacrifice. It is not the result of its own

> We must run this marathon of life on our own,
> reminding ourselves of the harsh truth
> that our victories and defeats can only be determined
> by the choices we make.

that impressed us, but the conviction and will to persevere and overcome difficulties and dreadful processes without an excuse. Furthermore, these examples of challenges inspire hope and give new motivation to someone else's dreams.

The waves on the beach do not come just once, but repeatedly and constantly rolling in and out, and so do our lives. Challenges and trials in life keep us on our toes. Tomorrow ahead of us often does not come true as we expected. We must run this marathon of life on our own, reminding ourselves of the harsh truth that our victories and defeats can only be determined by the choices we make.

The Vision of the Company and Me

Nothing changes until you put it into action

"How could you define the word 'Vision'?"

Pose this question to your coworkers, and you will see them agonizing to come up with a brilliant and fancy answer. The word "Vision" literally means the ability to see—eyesight; and the insight to know the future. An idiomatic English expression, "20/20 Vision," says you have good vision eyesight.

Numerous companies have their visions. The company's vision statement is concluded by its CEO, shareholders, executives, or consultants, putting a lot of thought and effort into it, and boiling it down to a simple sentence as a slogan. More specifically, the company's vision is "the future direction the company should go, the common language and driving force of the organization that sets out the calling of its members to make it happen." The vision inherently includes an understanding of the organization and communication, not only the direction of the company and the reason for being a member. The vision is something that everyone needs to embrace and pursue together; thus, the vision statement is simple, but the keywords present comprehensive terms.

Likewise, the vision is a lighthouse of the mind that guides a ship through a stormy night.

The step before the vision is a dream. The founders of companies would often start with a vague dream. Even a wanderer or homeless people probably had indefinite dreams back in the day.

A true dream is not a small personal thing like "I am going to save $1,000 before I retire" or "I will never be starved for next several days," but commonly, a big goal that is not easy to achieve. Dreams are vague in that regard. However, some people make them happen. On the other hand, others keep it in their heads for a while, like daydreaming, and then forget about it.

So how do you start from a vague dream to the ultimate way of realization—how do you turn your dream into concrete and finally achieve it?

Dr. Albert Einstein, famous for the theory of relativity, said, "Nothing happens until something moves." He referred to the observation of physical movement; nevertheless, it can be applied to our daily lives by being interpreted conceptually.

Vague is indistinct and fuzzy. In that sense, a vague dream is unlikely to change anything. You can only make a real change when you make your thoughts, concerns, repeated actions, and habits tangible.

In other words, you need to carefully think through your dream and what it contains and map it out clearly in your mind. At the same time, be determined to achieve and have a detailed plan for overcoming the challenges that will narrow the gap between your dreams and reality. Along the way, you also need to be realistic about and practically analyze the risks that may arise on the flip side: time, financial, and capability risks.

The dream is so ambitious that it requires sacrifices regarding choice and focus: less sleep, less leisure, etc. It is also the same

Guiding lights and shaping visions for your future!

concept as investing. If you start them haphazardly and without commitment, you're more likely to give up halfway through. That could be why you need to plan a fulfillment to make your dream a reality.

The dream fulfillment plan takes the following processes. Quantify your dreams first in an aspect of goals and draw up a timetable. Make sure to remind yourself of the dream project daily so that you can see it in your mind. Keeping a sheet of paper on your desk with your dreams written on it could be a good example.

Accompanying once you are ready, fuel your passion by imagining how happy you will be when your dreams are fulfilled while recognizing that your goals and actions will vary depending on your dreams' size and circumstances.

When your dream is clarified into a tangible vision, the next step is to flesh it out. Now that you have a direction of the vision, "where you want to go," you can decide how to get there, which is your mission.

Companies propose the "Mission Statement" together with the vision statement. The mission statement contains a specified way of how you will drive their vision forward. Again, the company's owner, president, and executives are putting their heads together and implicitly sharing their findings with their constituents and shareholders.

Another essential factor contained in the process is the core values. The core values are the things that are emphasized to keep members moving forward in unison. It is shared across the organization and generates momentum for work. Therefore, the core values shape a company's culture and bring the tone and energy.

When the mission and core values are shared and agreed upon within the organization around the vision, employees can internalize the company's values through systematic communication across functions and roles. Then, it establishes synergies between members, manifesting as a strong and sustained driving force to get work done.

The company's blueprint and framework, which could be superficial and conceptual, becomes visible through the above process. Then the company's work plans and projects are broken down into concrete, practical steps that lead to action.

The primary process of the action phase is to establish long-term and mid-term goals, followed by a year budget and short-term goals to execute the final action plan.

Certain factors should be considered and assumed when planning for the long, medium, or short-term, which are known as Key Critical Indicators (KCIs), Key Factors for Success (KFS),

> "
> When the mission and core values are shared and agreed upon within the organization around the vision, employees can internalize the company's values through systematic communication across functions and roles.
> "

or Key Performance Indicators (KPIs), substantially the same concepts.

KPIs are the key factors that are evaluated to deliver the expected results. They are metrics and indexes set as quantified targets, shared with the relevant members, and reinforced as something that must be considered and pursued in their work.

The KPIs should be considerably estimated and presented as the indexes or metrics that can express most effectively and evaluate performance after adequately understanding and analyzing the actual business records and internal and external environments.

An additional point to keep in mind is establishing a task owner and a deadline. When implementing a project, the owner, assistant, task contents, and final person in charge should be adopted and shared before the project begins so that the matter of responsibility is straightforward after the project is completed. Moreover, when multiple teams and managers' projects are jointly implemented, the deadlines should be clear to ensure harmony and work efficiency among teams. The larger and more competitive companies have the system in place, and the evaluation and rewards for results are objectively, quantitatively, and equitably applied.

For the fulfillment of the dream and effective execution of the vision, a company needs to share the same culture and values, build communication and consensus, and establish institutions and systems. Furthermore, it is necessary to provide continuous vision-oriented education, ongoing publicity to employees, and initiative leadership.

Some members are unconcerned about the vision being as meaningful as the executives because they think it has nothing to do with them or is unrealistic. There are numerous reasons behind this. It could be due to the vision or mission being fluffy, lacking authenticity, backward-looking, or not picturing return on investment (ROI) for the effort.

Some cynic members of the organization might complain, "What on earth is our vision?" or "There's no vision in my company." Then you ask back, "So, what's your vision?" They might often boggle or respond with a mundane answer to this question. It is impertinent to question or criticize the vision of others and your company when you don't even have your vision, which should be the most meaningful to you.

Summarizing the above process of starting with a dream, moving into a willing action, and finally coming to fruition can be said the following.

"Picture your dream first. Spread out your life's purpose over that dream, visualize your future in detail, and have the vision and mission ready. When you put the concept of time into your vision and mission, goals will emerge. When you break those goals down, you have plans. Now you can implement those plans and expect to see the results and accomplishments."

When you have your vision, mission, and values anchored in your life's purpose, you have a clear and concrete direction for any plan you make. Even if you hit a bump in the road and lose sight and way of your dreams, there is no need to get discouraged: your vision, mission, and core values will guide you back on track like a beacon.

How close are you to your purpose in life and where you want to be right now?

Gossip

Mary is pregnant with John's child?

Somehow in our lives, we are all bombarded with information in our daily lives. Especially in the age of the internet and social media, astronomical amounts of information are produced in a fraction of a second and circulated in real time. Amid it all, we are often caught up in a range of emotions: temporary joy, anger, sadness, pleasure—centered around the content, regardless of whether the information is true or not. While it would be nice to see every piece of information reflect the truth, the reality is that there is a lot of unethical and illegal distortion of facts.

From that perspective, let's look at the process and characteristics of gossip in an organization. The main subject of the gossip is usually about someone else and their situation. The original producer of the gossip often acts cowardly, hiding behind others while fostering a negative atmosphere. Gossip is usually reframed into an interesting story that can spark curiosity, and often involves slandering others. Furthermore, there is a sense of conviction and validity in the negative stories that the conspiracy theorists weave into them, making them very stimulating to listen to. Gossipers and the primary customers of gossip, are often driven by negative emotions such as greed, jealousy, insecurity, dissatisfaction, and anger, often fueled by inferiority complexes, competitiveness, and comparisons. Their "or not" or "whatever" attitudes can be devastating to the people in the organization who are the targets of their gossip.

In fact, while working at a US company, I often experienced situations like this. For example, I remember the case of Mary and John. Mary and John were coworkers who worked together in the same department and had a friendly relationship. One day, one of the other fellows came to me with a shocking story.

"Rumors are flying around the office that Mary is pregnant with John's child. I'm letting you know that dating a married man in the same company and being pregnant with his child is a serious matter under the company policy."

We then confidentially confronted the members involved and backtracked to the epicenter of the rumor, where we discovered that an employee in another department who hated Mary had cleverly fabricated and spread the story over several months.

The soap opera-like incident resulted in the woman who had slandered Mary got fired. Mary and John were transferred to

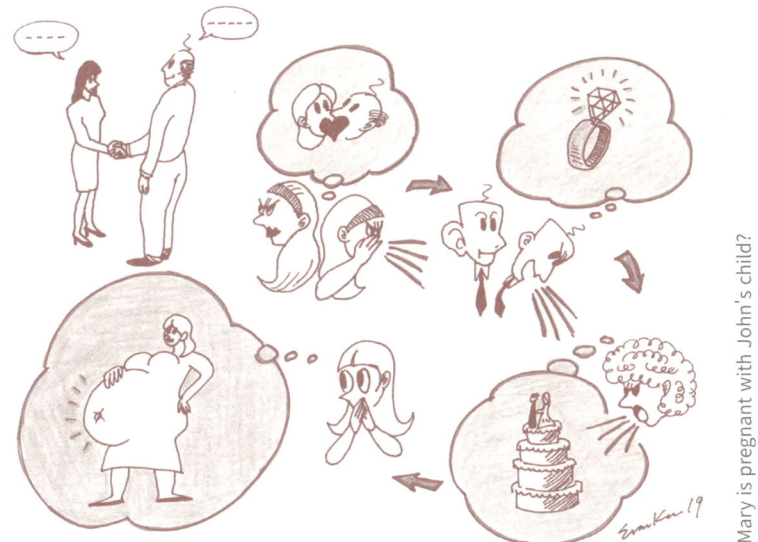

Mary is pregnant with John's child?

different departments. However, the gossip that followed caused Mary, who was competent and cheerful, to leave the company with mental distress.

With the recent advancement of technologies that have brought about the Fourth Industrial Revolution, we are inundated with unnecessary information, and fake information, which is untrue or distorted for ulterior motives or to capture attention, is causing people to become confused.

It spreads rapidly through individual online networks, and in the process, each piece of content becomes more and more mutated until it eventually becomes something else entirely. We're all too familiar with this kind of contamination.

The original producers of gossip and further disseminators of false information and malicious rumors do not hesitate about accusing and slandering specific people in a witch-hunt style. Some individuals suffer from extreme mental distress, suffering from depression, public avoidance, and panic disorders, which can lead to them taking their own lives. Murder, sexual assault, defamation, and other horrific crimes are already rampant in the online space without the need for a gun.

To varying degrees, something similar happens in companies. Employees who produce and circulate backstabbing gossip release resentment, anger, jealousy, humiliation, and frustration in secret accusations, often directed at unpleasant co-workers, competitors, or company policies and culture.

This gossip leads to negative relationships between employees, poor communication across departments, and low organizational morale, which ultimately impacts the company's productivity and competitiveness. To make matters worse, things that should be kept private become public.

What are the requirements for minimizing organizational gossip and its side effects?

First, smooth communication should be implemented in the

> "If the workplace operates with transparency and unity, and if management leads by example and communicates horizontally with employees to create a harmonious organizational atmosphere, it's harder to create backstabbing."

organization. Leadership must build a culture of transparent and consistent communication with all employees about strategies, policies, systems, and operations related to the company's future direction. The absence of this communication leaves members guessing and confused, with no actual understanding of the organization.

Second, the top-down, hierarchical, one-sided, and coercive atmosphere must be removed, as it is difficult for robust discussion and suggestions to flow freely. In fact, it's not uncommon for members with limited status and power to go along with their bosses to get along, and they may even engage in two-faced behavior, expressing their honest thoughts and feelings behind closed doors.

Third, internal clubs or private in-groups that are unrelated to the company should be avoided. An in-house organization that follows the company's policy is beneficial, meanwhile, the private organization is not based on the direction and needs of the company is related to their environment, and interests, and is often positioned as creating public opinion, supporting, and rallying power. These private organizations expect implicit alliances and cooperation from their members, and do not hesitate to alienate and frame someone when their plans go awry.

Most American companies have an individualistic, outgoing, and straightforward atmosphere. They respect each other's privacy, recognize the seriousness of discrimination in a multiracial society, and are less likely than in Korea to talk behind their backs because of the legal burden.

Instead, they make their arguments and opinions clear and openly criticize their opponents when necessary. They're used to excluding personal feelings. Even in the heat of an argument, they value their personal independence and the truth of a situation more than they value face and prestige.

However, in the case of Korean companies in the U.S., the presence of diverse races, generations, cultures, and values—including first, second, and third-generation Koreans, Americans, and other nationalities—can often result in challenges such as a lack of understanding, communication barriers, misunderstandings, and prejudice. Moreover, coupled with the superficial, introverted, metaphorical Korean mindset, often with comparisons based on age, status, wealth, etc., results in a reluctance to openly criticize and a tendency to keep negative thoughts and feelings to oneself, only to vent them later on to members who are not involved in the situation, creating and spreading gossip.

Key players who create a healthy, gossip-free organization, should include the chairman and executive team in the organization.

All members of an organization look to the vision and values of the company, as well as the actions and words of management, to gauge the quality and future of the company. So, if the workplace operates with transparency and unity, and if management leads by example and communicates horizontally with employees to create a harmonious organizational atmosphere, it's harder to create backstabbing. When people trust and work together, they're less likely to hide and cower, and less likely to try to get ahead by trampling on others.

Compensation and Motivation

It is all in the mindset

The philosophical question, "Do you live to eat or eat to live?" can be transformed into a practical one, "Do you live to earn or earn to live? Most people would probably answer "earn to live." But there are quite a few people who spend their entire lives focused on work and regret it in their old age.

Then how should you earn, and how much should you make, to live a decent and meaningful life?

In organizations, compensation is a key point of hiring terms, determined through post-interview offers and negotiations. Generally, salary is a quantification of the sum of an employee's capabilities; skills + work results + future potential. The salary is also a contract to pay an employee based on the sum of their competencies, with ongoing adjustments until the time of their leave.

The salary that a job candidate negotiates with a company before being hired has double sides. The candidate wants a salary level set based on their monetary value in the job market, their job-related urgency, and their financial comfort and sophistication. Companies, on the other hand, offer salaries that are based on a comparison of candidate skills to those at the same level in the organization, the hiring situation in the area, and the supply and demand for talent in the industry.

Once a candidate is hired, the salary is based on the company's structured HR practice and regular performance reviews from one's line manager and/or departmental colleagues. The company evaluates all employees relative to each other, focusing on job-related competencies and performance, accommodative capacity to organizational culture, work attitude, and personality, and adjusts salaries based on an overall assessment of their future value to the organization.

Most U.S. companies consider quantitative job performance, along with professional-based work competencies, to be important salary adjustment metrics when evaluating work. In contrast, Korean companies and some Korean-American companies in the U.S. often include qualitative metrics such as work attitude and the amount and length of work, in addition to job performance.

No method of salary adjustment is better than the other. What is important is to build a compensation management system that reflects the company's management philosophy, organizational culture, and core values. Ultimately, the company's goal is to keep employees happy, motivated, and financially secure with an optimally evaluated compensation management system.

In summary, a salary can be defined as a monetary contract between a company and its employees, a counter-payment that is made after a period of mutual negotiation, during which the needs and expectations of the company are assessed against the extent to which the employee is using one's capabilities and skills to fulfill the roles and tasks of the position.

It is also a challenging process that involves issues of relativity, subjectivity, and sensitivity, as it takes into account not only the competence, performance, and attitude of each employee on the job, but also the company's growth and financial stability, as well

as the hiring situation in the area where they work, the supply and demand for talent in the same industry, and equity between departments and among employees.

Let me share a story I have seen firsthand, and it happens often.

A member of the team, who was always motivated, performed above expectations and received a substantial pay rise, so he was satisfied with the company, grateful to his team leader, and worked even harder.

However, he became increasingly disgruntled, so I had an interview with him. The reason for being disgruntled was that he noticed that other team members with similar titles and experience, who were doing similar work, were being paid more than him, despite being less competent and performing less well.

He was originally positive, satisfied, and grateful in his relationship with the company, applying absolute and objective value standards. At some point, when he had something to compare it to, he applied relative and subjective value standards, turning positive into negative, satisfaction into dissatisfaction, and gratitude into complaint.

We had another case.

Three years ago, the company paid bonus to a member for outstanding work, performance, and attitude. The member's

> "Do not just assume the reason you work for an organization is because of the compensation. Think about your own motivators and future success at the organization, and you will get a more rewarding and meaningful work life."

satisfaction and motivation levels were very high. He achieved similar results two years ago as well. The evaluation was awarded with the same level of bonus as last year, which was sufficiently motivating. However, a year ago, he performed reasonably well but not as well as expected, so the evaluation was an above-average with decent bonus that was lower than two or three years ago but higher than other members.

The rewards received in the past two years became the minimum baseline of what he was entitled to, and the person who had expressed gratitude and satisfaction is now feeling uncomfortable with the rewards of anything less than that, regardless of the reason.

A person's value to a company can be expressed in terms of their job title and duties, responsibilities and authority, salary and compensation, etc. Among these, quantitative metrics like salary are important and essential.

The sense of fulfillment, happiness, and value you experience in your work life is influenced not only by your salary but also by metaphysical and qualitative factors. Some of the wise people in the company are valued for their ability to understand, accept, and overcome difficult, challenging, unfair, and unreasonable situations, differentiating them from those who live their lives in the company on a quantitative basis only.

Even if there is no perfect company or the right company for you, maintaining a positive attitude, contentment, and gratitude can open up new opportunities and positions as you work through challenges.

In an aspect of organizational management, of course, compensation is the most important contributor to a positive organizational climate and employee self-motivation, but it is not everything.

A positive organizational atmosphere becomes visible when sharing company vision and culture, excellent leadership from executives and managers, efficient and effective communication and decision-making structures, understanding of evaluation systems and satisfaction with job training. The values and mindset of employees are nonignorable factors. If employees view the company as a relationship of dominance and subordination, as a means to get their needs met, and as a paycheck in exchange for labor, their work life cannot be satisfied.

Also, while salary levels have a significant impact on voluntary motivation, its sustainability is difficult to guarantee, because employees typically think of pay as a relative value based on comparison and competition rather than an absolute value.

We all need income to survive. However, if we establish the why and how of our work life before the level and content of our salary, we can move beyond merely worrying about making a living and also find happiness. Everything depends on the mind.

So, do not just assume the reason you work for an organization is because of the compensation. Think about your own motivators and future success at the organization, and you will get a more rewarding and meaningful work life.

Diversity and Inclusion

I am Mr. Manager and not just a manager!

When evaluating and managing employees, U.S. companies focus on skills and performance, with an employee's title or position not being considered a key criterion. In contrast, titles are more of a concern in Korean companies or Korean-American companies in the U.S. The reason for this difference can be found in cultural and language differences.

The English have fewer honorifics and titles, so when you address someone in a U.S. company, you generally address them by their first name, not their last name, regardless of their title.

In Korean companies, people are called by their last name with a title at the end. For example, "Kim + Manager + Sir." Surely, Korean companies are now trying to eliminate the organizational side effects of the title system as Korean annual salary system (flexible & negotiable) and team concept take hold. Nonetheless, the social sentiment and Confucian background in Korea make it difficult to implement and we often see trial-and-error situations.

At a Korean-American company in the U.S. where I once worked, a conversation between two Korean managers led to a formal complaint to HR that the older manager was ignored because the younger manager did not address him with a polite title form. The younger manager argued against the older manager that the Korean custom of addressing the older manager as "Sir." was inappropriate in the company, even though they had the same title, tenure and salary.

This issue can seem simple or burdensome depending on one's perspective, but it is definitely not something to be taken lightly. No one can say that an organization is wrong for only calling people by their title without using the honorific "Sir," but in Korean society and companies, it is a very important issue related to self-esteem and pride. So, the HR team took the extra effort and time to resolve the situation amicably and mutually.

The Korean cultural context and background give vertical organizations an advantage. These organizations operate in a military-like, with a stable chain of command, clear responsibilities, and well-defined authority structures. On the other hand, such an organizational culture can be highly bureaucratic, with prestige and face value. Thus, organizations need to move faster to horizontal cultural groups to break through the bureaucracy and become competitive in a performance-based organization.

Recently, Korean companies have been going through a process of coexisting with social changes and the young generation's mindset, which aligns with the existing Korean sentiment and background. Transforming an organization without fully reflecting its institutions, culture, values, and history can have unexpected side effects, and many Korean companies have reverted to the way they were before the change.

When I am faced with a member who cares so much about title and position that it's almost like their reason for being in the organization, I often make jokes like,

I am Mr. Manager and not just a manager!

"You are called 'General Manager, Mr. Kim' at Company A, but you go to local flea market now and shout out, 'I'm General Manager, Mr. Kim from Company A.' They might think you're crazy."

It is simple why the title or position people are fighting for in the company can become worthless in the flea market. The radius of people's social lives is not as wide or as big as we think. We are realizing who we are as a society in a very limited time, place, and circumstance.

The reality is that many Korean-American companies in the United States are "multi-ethnic" and "multi-cultural" organizations. First and second-generation Koreans coexist with Americans and other immigrants of all ages and backgrounds, creating a mix of Korean and American cultures, sentiments, and values. Therefore, it is important to consider a variety of circumstances and factors to build a thriving organizational culture.

A multi-ethnic, multicultural organization with a diverse workforce can often feel like an alien group, making a shared company vision and common goals even more important than in a typical company.

To make it happen, multi-ethnic and multicultural organizations must build company policies, organizational

> If a company sensitively and carefully considers even the very minor impacts of title issue like "Sir" on the organization, it can certainly create a global company where diversity and inclusivity coexist harmoniously.

charts, hierarchies, human resources systems, and work policies and procedures that respect diversity. For organizations and employees with heterogeneous attributes, the key is to carefully consider the complex and diverse issues that are not inherent in homogeneous organizations.

When cooking, no matter how great the ingredients we use and the special recipes we apply, if we don't have the right balance of flavors, we won't have a delicious meal. The same concept applies to people management in organizations. We need to recruit a diverse group of people with great knowledge, skills, and attitudes from across society. Then, build an organization that communicates, understands, and collaborates harmoniously to create a competitive organization, like delicious food.

Perhaps the perfect organization is an unrealistic ideal. If a company's CEO, executives, and managers genuinely practice respect, understanding, compromise, care, and sharing, allowing people to work together organically, the organization can move forward collectively toward its vision and common goals, even in a multi-ethnic, multi-cultural world.

If a company sensitively and carefully considers even minor issues, such as the use of titles like "Sir", it can support a global company where diversity and inclusivity coexist harmoniously.

Communication and Listening

A king observes and listens
with two ears, ten eyes, and one heart

I used to work for an organization whose primary customers were women and, whose workforce was also predominantly female. I was responsible for people management and organizational dynamics as a whole, so I spent a lot of time in one-on-one meetings with employees for a variety of reasons. I remember going the extra mile when meeting with female employees.

I always had a stack of tissues on my desk. Many of the women who came to see me talked about difficulties and uncomfortable issues rather than happy things, and they often ended up in tears because they couldn't control their emotions during the conversation. So I got into the habit of checking for tissues first whenever a woman came to see me.

I have conducted many meetings, but what makes me particularly nervous is when an employee enters without any explanation or context, displaying only tears and sobbing or showing anger and excitement. In each case, my priority is to create a comfortable atmosphere so that the employee can fully communicate, which requires respect for the employee, gentleness, and listening with compassion and empathy.

We often use the word "communication" but unfortunately, the importance of its word is being diluted by overuse. Many conflicts in our daily and social lives are caused by miscommunication. One of the leading causes of divorce is communication issues and the same applies to conflicts between people within a company.

Communication can be broken down into five elements; the sender and receiver of the message, the content of the message and how it's delivered (verbally, by phone, email, etc.), and finally, the response or feedback to the message sender.

In addition to language, nonverbal elements such as facial expressions, posture, tone of voice, and gestures can be used to communicate your thoughts, intentions, and feelings more clearly, and can be strategically planned.

The basic and most obvious method I use is to follow the so-called 5W 1H principal (who, to whom, what, why, when, where, and how). Utilizing these aspects properly can help you get your point across in a straightforward way.

Organizational communication is often professional, not emotional, like a novel or essay. The ultimate goal is to ensure that everyone understands your message in a timely manner. Therefore, it is important to establish effective methods and procedures for communicating key information to your audience. For instance, delivering a message about organizing a meeting involves the following steps.

① Decision on who lead the meeting (identify the most appropriate person, including yourself)
② Selection of message recipients (specific individuals or a general audience)
③ Organizing the content of your message (articulate the background and purpose persuasively)
④ Anticipating and preparing for the recipient's response
⑤ Defining the final objective and expected outcome of the meeting (varies depending on whether it is for training, education, announcements, decision-making, etc.)
⑥ Determining the time, place, and method of delivering the message
⑦ Strategic planning to maximize message appeal (e.g., combining internal communications with marketing)

You need to be thoughtful in a company when making an

announcement, a written proposal, or an email communication. The purpose is clear. You want to make your communication as simple, clear, and convincing as possible so that the person you are communicating with can easily understand it in a short amount of time and, if possible, agree with what you are saying.

From that perspective, you should always consider the other person's point of view when preparing your communication and then strategically modify it as necessary, because when you consider what the other person might be thinking instead of just your own perspective, you're more likely to find a solution that will convince them. This is a long-standing principle of mine when preparing for communications. There's another reason for its importance. When I listen to or observe a meeting or presentation organized by a coworker, or receive an email from a business associate, I can indirectly assess not only the content but also the level of preparation and the individual's, competence. This principle means that the meetings, presentations, and emails I organize are always being observed and evaluated by someone.

It is common sense, but one of the most important and difficult parts of communication is listening, which symbolically explains the fact that we have one mouth and two ears. The mouth is used for a variety of purposes, including speaking,

A king observes and listens with two ears, ten eyes, and one heart.

THE ART OF LISTENING

eating, and breathing. The ears are used solely for listening. That makes listening special.

The Chinese character for listening has two meanings, depending on the character. The first listening (敬聽) means "listen with respect," while the second listening (傾聽) means "listen with attention." The Chinese character for "hearing" is a combination of the characters for "ear (耳)," "king (王)," "ten (十)," "eye (目)," "one (一)," and "heart (心)," and it means "A king observes and listens with two ears, ten eyes, and one heart."

I do not know how the character "hearing (聽)" came to be, but it has a unique and persuasive meaning the more we look into it.

When I think about listening, I am reminded of the Talmudic

quote, "Knowledge seeks to speak, and wisdom seeks to listen." This sentence resonated with me, and I realized that in my daily and social life, listening is much harder than speaking.

It is common for multiple people to hear the same message at the same time, but they often understand the same message differently. Why do these miscommunications occur?

First, they tend to interpret every situation through the lens of their own position, and interests, which means they hear or see only what aligns with what they want to hear in a conversation.

Secondly, it is because people lack interest and affection for the other person, so they listen in one ear and let it go out the other. They make eye contact, nod their heads, and act like they are listening, but thinking something else in their mind.

The third is a lack of respect for the other person's situation and feelings. I often use the following points about respect in my employee training sessions.

The English word "understanding" can be broken down into "under" and "standing," which can be interpreted as "to stand under." In this case, "standing under" means humbling yourself, which is a concept of mutual respect. With this attitude, you can truly listen and understand what the other person is saying.

Fourth is that people do not understand the difference between "low context" and "high context." Here, "context," which means context is used as a paraphrase rather than a literal translation.

"Low context" is when the message is expressed directly, as it is in your head. "High context" is when the message is expressed indirectly, as in the so-called "reading between the lines," leaving it up to the listener to understand your intentions and thoughts. "High context" can include facial expressions, gestures, and mood.

Typically, the United States is considered a "low context" culture, while Korea is viewed as a "high context" culture.

In "low context," the words or message is the expression itself, so if you understand the other person's words properly, you will fully communicate. When Americans communicate, they solely focus on the story rather than paying attention to the five senses. This is also evident in American culture and history. They are personal, assertive, direct, and clear in their opinions, so the content, tone, and emotions tend to be reflected in their conversations.

On the other hand, in "high context," not only language but also non-verbal behaviors are included in the message, so it must be understood and analyzed holistically to understand the other person's words or messages. Koreans use all five senses in their speech and messages. Korean sentiment is collective and communal, and conversations are often implicit and indirect. Facial expressions and gestures are also used as communication tools.

Then how do you communicate and listen effectively in a U.S. company or a U.S.-Korean company?

First, you need to set the tone for a comfortable conversation. When you start a conversation, you need to minimize awkwardness and ambiance with a soft expression and demeanor that lets the other person's guard down.

Once you are in the middle of the conversation, you should periodically make "eye contact" with the person. In the U.S., eye contact means that you are interested in what they are saying and what they are trying to tell you and that you are genuinely listening. Avoiding eye contact suggests that you are not confident in the conversation or that you are not being honest.

Due to cultural differences, Koreans in the U.S. often feel uncomfortable with eye contact. This is because Korean culture considers it impolite to stare at someone older or of higher status. In this case, you can achieve the same effect as eye contact by looking at the person's nose.

You should also pay close attention and express genuine interest when the other person is speaking; otherwise, the conversation may lose its momentum. For example, if you

> "
> The Chinese character for "hearing" is a combination of the characters for "ear (耳)," "king (王)," "ten (十)," "eye (目)," "one (一)," and "heart (心)," and it means "A king observes and listens with two ears, ten eyes, and one heart."
> "

look at your watch or look away for even a moment during a conversation, the other person may take it as "I'd like to end the conversation" or "I'm not interested in what you have to say."

So, you need to respond with a "I see" or nodding gesture during the conversation. It is also good to use some parts of the conversation to ask short questions. For example, if someone says, "I recently traveled to Seoul," could be followed up with, "I was there last year as well, what did you enjoy most about the food?" to keep the conversation flowing.

However, while "I see" or "I understand" is an acceptable response to show that you understand what the other person is saying, be careful with "I agree" or "You're right," which can be misconstrued as a promise to agree with them.

Next, you need to be patient and respectful toward, the other person to fully hear them out. Be aware not to show any signals or attitudes that indicate what the other person is saying does not make sense or does not have value, and you want to quickly end the conversation. In addition, you cannot listen to someone in a way of bombarding them with advice or talking down to them. If you listen with respect for them as a human being, regardless of their position or level of competence, they will appreciate the genuine connection, and you will have a much better chance of getting through the actual task at hand.

Next, it is crucial to be mindful of your words, as you cannot take back what you've said once it's out. We often overlook these in real-life conversations. Avoid making promises or lying to save face, as this is a liability. We also need to eradicate negative and destructive conversations that put emotion ahead of rational judgment, leading to humiliation, hostility, and even legal action. Pointing fingers and reprimanding someone, especially in a group activity, has many negative consequences. A straightforward conversation can quickly turn into a discussion full of negative emotions like insults, belittlement, envy, or jealousy. It might also shift to arguments about tone, appearance, or personal matters, causing the original point to be lost. This can cause significant problems for both parties and their organizations.

The last thing to keep in mind is that sensitive information requiring confidentiality in various aspects should only be shared with the relevant individuals. If confidential information is leaked and spread through gossip, trust between people in an organization can be broken and hard to rebuild.

In organizations, communication and active listening are the most important and essential elements for performing tasks, and this is true for American companies as well. Although most people are well aware of this, there is often a tendency to approach it complacently and with a self-centered perspective. As a result, misunderstandings, communication breakdowns, deteriorating relationships, and ultimately decreased productivity continue to occur within organizations. While many companies prioritize products, services, systems, revenue, and more to stay competitive, there is a significant lack of attention and effective problem-solving when it comes to functional managers' communication skills and their ability to establish relationships within the organization.

The primary purpose of communication is to have positive exchanges—professional, social, and relational matters—and part of that is to share, feel, and be present in each life.

We hope you are now reminded of the importance of good communication and listening, and that you are equipped with a clear head and a genuine heart to move yourself and your organization forward.

Efficiency and Effectiveness

I don't spend or waste time; I use it wisely or invest it

Efficiency and effectiveness are important and commonly used concepts in the natural sciences, as well as in business administration and real-world business and organizational management. This is a topic I address in my organization's training programs on time management.

Efficiency and effectiveness are fundamental concepts in business process design that everyone in an organization should leverage, especially because they are not only quantitative but also interpersonal.

A simple definition of efficiency and effectiveness is that efficiency means "doing things right," while effectiveness means "doing the right things." To be more specific, efficiency focuses on "process and method" as "doing what you plan to do in an appropriate course or way," while effectiveness focuses on "results" as "doing what is required and producing the best possible outcome.

For example, let's say there are two ice cream companies, A and B. Company A has a great manufacturing process, and its employees are well versed in the process and can produce 1 million units per day, quickly, accurately, and with excellent quality. Company B has a similar quality to Company A, but its manufacturing process is more complex. Its employees are less specialized, and its total production is half of Company A. Company A ships its ice cream during the winter season, while Company B ships during the summer season. Most likely, Company A sold less ice cream due to seasonal factors, while Company B sold all of its ice cream despite producing only half as much as Company A.

Let me demonstrate efficiency and effectiveness incorporating the above situation. Company A is efficient because it went through the process of doing its job properly but is ineffective because its decision to sell in the winter didn't produce the best results. On the other hand, Company B is less efficient than Company A in terms of process, but more effective in terms of outcome.

In conclusion, from a business perspective, Company B has executed better management than Company A. The ultimate purpose of a business is to create the best performance, no matter how good the process is, if the outcome is poor, the purpose of the business may lose its significance. However, even though the process is relatively poor, if the outcome shows the best performance, it meets the purpose of the business. Therefore, effectiveness should take precedence over efficiency in business considerations.

As an additional example to demonstrate, a professional soccer team and a local soccer club are playing a friendly match. The goal of a soccer match is to win, and achieving that requires scoring goals. The professional soccer team fires off a dozen or so powerful shots, following up with some brilliant dribbling and precise passing, but unfortunately, they did not score a single goal. But the local soccer club, despite sloppy dribbling and inaccurate passing, took advantage of two or three opportunities to score two goals and eventually win the game. The process was inefficient, but the result was effective.

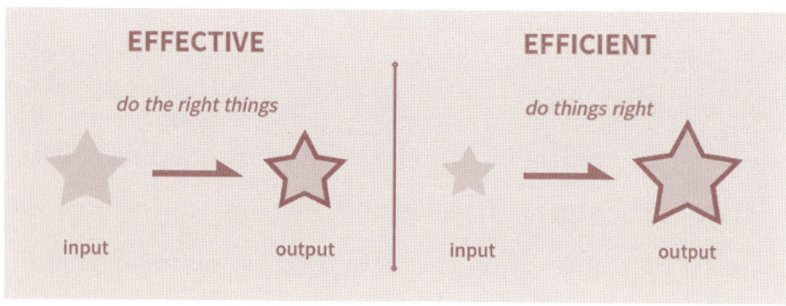

Do the right things and do things right!

In organizations, including companies, most people in mid-level management and below focus on getting things done. In many cases, there is an emphasis on efficiency—the process of getting things done—rather than on effectiveness, the outcome of getting things done. But senior managers, including executives, are judged by their outcomes, and their companies live and die by them, so they emphasize effectiveness over efficiency.

The truth is, that the people who get recognized in a company are the ones who produce outcomes. Does not matter how organized you are or how hardworking you are, if you are not contributing to the company's ultimate goals like revenue and profit, you are not going to be an indispensable member of the team.

However, emphasizing effectiveness at the expense of efficiency will have side effects. That is why a good balance of efficiency and effectiveness is required. With that in mind, let's look at the key concepts for improving the efficiency of your work processes.

The first principle is "once." Whenever possible, work should be completed in one go, as doing it two or three times unnecessarily wastes time and money.

Second principle is "simple." The procedures and content of your work should be as simple and straightforward as possible, because the more complicated things get, the harder it is to understand and the more effort it takes.

The Third principle is "same." The work needs to be standardized and build systems to ensure that everyone follows the same procedures and methods when doing their work. If a process is not standardized, it will inevitably result in lower quality, lower productivity, and lower efficiency.

Conversely, when you excel in all three of these aspects, you will achieve the "speedy" effect of completing tasks faster and "saving effect" of conserving time, money, and effort.

To summarize we can use the phrase "1O & 4S." "1O" stands for "once" and "4S" represents "simple," "same," "saving," and "speedy." Together, this means: "do it once, keep it simple, ensure consistency (same), prioritize savings, and aim for speed."

It is a clear and logical concept that is easy to understand. However, in the real world, this often does not apply for a variety of reasons; "I've been too busy to think about it," "My boss always wants things done his way," "It has been working, so why bother changing it?" and so on. Even when we recognize the need for improvement and change, we often revert to the old processes and procedures, leaving poor performance unchanged.

For example, I once worked in the U.S. office of a large Korean firm, where I was responsible for holistically improving existing business processes in the U.S. office for management transformation. At that time, a management transformation technique called Business Process Reengineering (BPR) was in vogue. The biggest challenge in improving business processes for transformation was surprisingly with the department heads. They were complacent and inert, influenced by a mix of overconfidence from past successes and a fear of failure.

When talking about efficiency, it is helpful to remember the carpenter's principle. A carpenter cuts and shapes wood to make furniture and other structures, so they focus their attention on measuring and sawing the width, length and thickness of wood according to a drawing or design.

If a carpenter cuts wood differently from the drawing or design, it can cause problems. If he cuts enough wood, he still has a chance to re-cut it and only needs to spend a little bit of time and effort again. However, if he cuts it too short, the wood cannot be used for its intended purpose, resulting in wasted time, effort, and money. That is why carpenters live by the mantra "measure twice, cut once" when sawing.

The carpenter's principle suggests that valuing the process often leads to better, the results. This exemplifies how efficiency can drive effectiveness.

Efficiency and effectiveness at work involve considering,

managing, and discussing work-related goals, objectives, procedures, and methods. A key element that cannot be overlooked is managing both individual time and the team's overall work time. The efficiency and effectiveness of your work are greatly influenced by the standards you set for managing and organizing both your time and the company's time.

Time is fair to everyone. But we often say we did not have enough time to get things done for a variety of reasons. That is why it is important to create find time in the moment. To effectively manage and organize our time, we must first allocate time to reflect on it.

From that perspective, establishing the following concepts in your mind will help you utilize your time more positively and productively.

"I don't spend or waste time, but I use or invest it."

This concept shifts your perspective on time from being passive and reactive to being active and proactive.

To become an effective time manager who maximizes the value of your time, it is essential to analyze your daily routine in detail. From waking up to going to bed, you should carefully plan the purpose, goals, and details of what you need to do and how you will do. From that, you need to quantify and minimize the various wasted idle time, and you need to refine your routine to ensure that you are utilizing close to 100% of your time, excluding sleep.

I would like to share some examples of workers whose time management practices you can learn from.

> On an ordinary day, he wakes up after a good sleep and heads out to work during rush hour. Naturally, his mind and body are slowly wearing down with tension, impatience, and irritation as he faces a hectic traffic situation.
>
> He arrives at the office just in time, turns on his computer, and heads straight to the office pantry for a cup of coffee. He greets his coworkers and kills time with unnecessary small talk. Then he stops by the restroom to defecate. After a considerable amount of time passes, he starts to work. He puts aside tasks that require careful consideration due to time constraints and prioritizes those with imminent deadlines. His desk is a mess, but he has no time to tidy it up. When a meeting starts, he attends half-reluctantly. Yet again, he sits in the meeting room without contributing.
>
> In the meantime, his lunch break is coming up. After eating at an off-site restaurant with his coworkers, he spends all his lunch break and returns to the office.
>
> He sits down and resumes his work, chasing away afternoon slump after a meal. Slowly, he kicks off into his work, tackling his assignments and requests, and before he knows it, it's time to go home. Despite working intensely for two or three hours in the

afternoon, he feels like he has been working all day. As one by one his coworkers leave the office, he puts off until tomorrow what he should have finished today and joins them on their way out the door. He continued to delude himself into believing that he worked hard after hours, justifying his decision to watch video content as a reward. Then, as sleepiness set in, he goes to bed, concluding the day with the thought "I was so busy again today!"

Next, a particularly important concept in internal time management is prioritization. Prioritization can be defined as determining the order of importance and timeliness of several tasks based on objective and logical criteria.

When setting priorities in a company, we start by listing our internal challenges and clearly defining the purpose, goals, reason, and desired outcomes. Then, we organize the tasks in order of importance to ensure their successful achievement.

Above all, timeliness must be considered. Regardless of how important a task may be, it cannot take precedence over one with an imminent deadline.

While this is an extreme example, if there is a fire in the office, you need to put it out or evacuate. In other words, your priorities are likely to shift based on timeliness.

These priorities are easy to organize visually with a coordinate plane.

First, draw a coordinate plane with importance as the horizontal axis (x-axis) and timeliness as the vertical axis (y-axis). Things to the right of the center point are more important, and things to the left are less. Things toward the top are more urgent, and things toward the bottom are less urgent.

When applied simultaneously, more prioritized and urgent tasks are in the top-right corner, more prioritized and less urgent tasks are in the bottom-right corner, and less prioritized and more urgent tasks are in the top-left corner, less prioritized and less urgent tasks are in the bottom-left corner.

Once tasks are organized by priorities and timeliness, you should aim to eliminate low-priority tasks from the bottom left and increase focus on high-proirity ones at the bottom right. In addition, urgent tasks in the upper left and upper right quadrants should be minimized regardless of their importance. Urgent work depends on a variety of factors, including project deadlines, employee capabilities, work processes, and more. However, the bottom line is that an excessive amount of urgent work negatively impacts overall performance, reducing efficiency and increasing employee stress. Therefore, it is crucial to minimize unavoidable urgent tasks and create a work environment that prioritizes important tasks.

Another valuable concept for internal time management is the

"80:20 rule," which is also known as the "Pareto Principle."

In the late 19th century, Italian economist Pareto found that about 80% of all taxes in Italy were paid by the top 20% of earners by income level. He studied the correlation between 80% and 20% and concluded that in most cases, 80% of the overall effect results from the top 20% of the causes. If you apply the 80:20 rule to restaurants, the top 20% of the menu often accounts for about 80% of the restaurant's revenue.

The 80:20 rule works just as well in the work. The top 20% of your work by importance represents the quality and quantity of about 80% of your work. Paradoxically, this also means that the bottom 80% of your task only affects about 20% of your outcomes. So, if you thoroughly analyze your entire task and focus on the top 20% of your work by priority, you can expect to perform at least 80% of your work.

Delegating tasks is also an essential strategy for managing your time wisely. Delegating a task implies using resources from someone else, such as a coworker, to execute the task. It's important to distinguish delegation from transfer. Delegation means you are still accountable for the outcome of a task, whereas transfer means you relinquish involvement and responsibility for that task. Some managers mistake delegation for transfer, and when things go wrong, they blame the other

> The concepts of efficiency and effectiveness quantitatively emphasize the economic value of maximizing the return on tangible and intangible investments.

person for it.

Ideal task delegation enables managers to focus on higher-priority tasks that drive productivity while ensuring delegates have meaningful experiences with their new tasks. Additionally, unnecessary tasks should be identified and either reduced or eliminated where possible.

Key element of time management at the company or organizational level, beyond individual efforts, is assigning task owners and setting deadlines.

In a company, while some tasks are handled individually, most projects require collaboration with other employees or teams. Therefore, it is essential to designate a task owner and a deadline as a professional commitment. Being clear about this at the start of a task helps prevent miscommunication, blame-shifting, and strained relationships, ensuring everyone works together to meet a shared deadline.

We have explored the concepts of efficiency and effectiveness and discussed their application to both your personal life and professional work.

The concepts of efficiency and effectiveness quantitatively emphasize the economic value of maximizing the payback on tangible and intangible investments. This can be seen through the economic term Return On Investment (ROI). ROI, also known as return on invested capital or payback, is the primary reason for economic activity. The formula for calculating ROI is the total amount of output, such as goods or services, divided by the total amount of input, such as raw materials or labor.

The goal of economic activity is to achieve the best possible outcome with minimal resources. Inputs include tangible elements like raw materials, labor, and costs, as well as intangible values such as beliefs, passion, and responsibility. Outputs encompass tangible results like goods, services, and revenue, alongside intangible outcomes such as happiness, fulfillment, and unity.

Manage your inputs effectively, and the desired outputs will naturally follow. Just as in life, when we efficiently incorporate exercise, care, and dreams into our daily routines, we can achieve our goals of health, respect, and happiness.

Good Company

The company is more than just a livelihood

While working in the United States, I held an executive role overseeing people management and organizational dynamics, during which I interviewed and hired numerous Americans and Koreans. Over the course of a year, I reviewed hundreds of resumes, gaining valuable experience in effectively interviewing candidates regardless of their race, age, gender, or experience.

Typically, job applicants approach interviews with confidence, believing they are the right fit in terms of expertise, experience, attitude, personality. Those who successfully navigate the process often begin their careers with high ambition and determination. However, it is not uncommon for some of those who start their careers with such enthusiasm to leave the organization. In my experience, individuals with less organizational and social experience, coupled with a strong personality, tend to have a higher the rate of early departure.

I've conducted numerous exit interviews with the departing

or terminated employees, striving to listen to their reasons with objectivity and fairness. Their honest feedback about whether the process was reasonable and equitable can provide valuable insights to enhance the organization's operations and culture.

Through interviews with the employees, I have gathered various reasons for leaving an organization. Skepticism about the company's vision and growth, conflict with a supervisor or colleague, and dissatisfaction with the company's culture and values were the reasons. More recently, it is worth noting that millennials and the next generation have been cited as reasons for leaving the workforce: seeking a forward-thinking work environment, clarified job responsibilities and authority, career advancement, and better pay and benefits.

So, what does a "good company" look like in the eyes of employees, including the next generation? Interviews consistently revealed that a good company is financially stable, guided by desirable values, vision, and mission. It fosters an organizational culture of respect, fairness, and trust, with consistent horizontal and vertical communication among employees, enabling both the company and its workforce to grow together.

In these good companies, not only management but also employees are aware of the organization's goals and work in the

The company is more than just a livelihood.

same direction.

All employees take ownership, lead by example, and make sacrifices, just like the CEO. They naturally have a sense of pride and loyalty to the company, and communication and relationships between employees are smooth, creating positive synergy through mutual understanding and consultation.

People of all tendencies and backgrounds work at companies across many different cultures. And people are the most important part of a company. However, a company's competitiveness relies on more than just employees' knowledge, skills, and attitudes. Management performance also depends on the company's values, vision, culture, philosophy, and relationships among executives and managers.

No matter how talented your employees are, a company cannot thrive if it allows situations like the following to occur.

Employees who spend work hours chatting and browsing social media; self-centered employees who waste company resources like supplies; leaders who dominate, demand special treatment, and use insulting language without hesitation; and leaders who engage in sexual harassment under the guise of joking, without any sense of guilt. A cold and disconnected team atmosphere where laughter has disappeared, and communication has broken down. A self-defensive team atmosphere that blames other departments. An organizational culture where complaints and dissatisfaction with the company prevail, and gossip or slander about employees is widespread. A passive culture where employees blindly follow their bosses' instructions during meetings, marked by silence and a lack of engagement. Of course, these companies likely did not start out with negative intentions either.

Intangible factors like leadership, communication, relationships, and attitudes are more influential than tangible factors like capabilities, systems, regulations, and products.

Companies are for-profit organizations made up of a diverse group of people. People contribute their skills and experience to the company and are paid for it. As a result, many people in the

> "
> Even the good companies have ups and downs.
> Thus, it is good to have a mindset
> that sees work as more than a means of livelihood
> but a place where you can find gratitude and reward.
> "

workforces seem to view their jobs as merely a means of making a living and a tool for advancement, which is why they prioritize high salaries and senior positions.

The principle of metric, quantitative evaluation, and a give-and-take dynamic has long been the foundation of the employer-employee relationship in the U.S. As a result, employees do not hesitate to change jobs if they believe the new workplace offers better opportunities or conditions than their current one.

Across all generations and within various political, economic, social, and cultural contexts, we rely on income from our work to make ends meet. However, the career we build with the company we aspire to work for won't necessarily last forever on our own terms. The symbiotic relationship between an employee and employer can end at any time—whether through retirement, voluntary departure, or termination by the company. This makes it crucial to manage our work lives effectively, as they encompass a significant portion of our productive years. Ideally, we would all like to feel fully engaged, recognized, and rewarded in our roles at work.

But in my experience, the world is not easy to navigate, and even the good companies face their ups and downs. Therefore, it is valuable to adopt a mindset that views work as more than just a means of livelihood. Instead, consider it a place where you can discover gratitude and personal fulfillment.

We spend a significant portion of our lives working. If the sole reason for your work is merely to make a living, it's likely that dissatisfaction will follow throughout your life.

However, even though corporate life can be challenging, finding happiness and peace within it gives it its own intrinsic value. By treating work as an integral and valuable part of your life rather than separating it from your livelihood, you can uncover meaningful life values and true fulfillment.

From "Myself" to "We" and "Together"

The whole world is rotten!

As part of my role, I have developed a habit of observing people. This involves objectively noticing employees' behaviors, facial expressions, and attitude—not as a form of investigation or surveillance, but as essential preparation for performing my jobs effectively and smoothly. By paying close attention, I gain insights into their characteristics, personalities, psychology, and thought processes, enabling me to communicate from multiple perspectives and foster stronger relationships. From this perspective, psychology and social psychology, which examine human nature and behavior within society and organizations, can be valuable tools for improving communication and building relationships.

People typically exhibit a coherent alignment between their thoughts, spoken words direct speech, and indirect gestures and facial expressions. For example, some gestures defy gravity, and others conform to it. Defying gravity by raising your arms to the sky or giving a thumbs-up expresses confidence, success, and comfort. Conversely, gravitationally compliant behavior, such as slumped shoulders or thumbs-down, is an expression of a lack of confidence, failure, and depression.

Another example is rubbing your neck or fiddling with your tie or necklace during a meeting or conversation, which can indicate feelings of anxiety, discomfort, or worry.

By observing and analyzing these direct expressions in words and actions, along with indirect expressions such as gestures, facial expressions, eye contact, voice, and tone of voice, it becomes easier to understand the person's personality and psychology. Moreover, it has a positive effect on communication and can help you establish rapport or gain a strategic advantage.

For a long time, I have been working out at the gym in the early morning before work, and I have observed various people. One observation about treadmills comes to mind. After a treadmill workout, people often break out in a sweat, but their reactions vary. And I have categorized them into four groups based on their behavior.

There are four types of users: those who wipe before and after use with sanitary wipes, those who don't wipe before but wipe after use, those who wipe before but not after use, and those who wipe neither before nor after use.

Which category do you think you belong to? Naturally, people with the best attitudes fall into the first category, while those with the worst attitudes are in the fourth. But what about the third category? Do you ever think that might be acting selfishly? And how about people the second category? Personally, I feel a warm, human connection with people in the second category, which makes them more likable to me than the seemingly perfect individuals in the first category. Of course, this doesn't mean that the second category is better than the first.

Let's apply this to our daily work life, where some of your coworkers seem perfect, like the first category, but they can be somewhat intimidating in terms of relationships. The

The whole world is rotten!

fourth category is likely to be avoided in terms of work and relationships.

The third category looks selfish or egocentric, which can make other members wary. You can establish relationships and make yourself known out of necessity, gaining short-term acceptance in the organization. However, in the long run, the negative perceptions from your peers are likely to spread throughout the organization.

The second category, on the other hand, consists of people you'd want to get along with because they are down-to-earth, caring about others more than themselves, and have a genuine human side. This is why their "personality" stands out in a positive light.

Of course, this situation is just one example that excludes work capabilities, so it cannot be used to draw general conclusions. However, it may hold significance from a human perspective. A popular reality TV show, 「Undercover Boss」, illustrates this idea well. The show features companies of various types and sizes, with the CEO of each company disguising their identity and joining as a new employee to work alongside staff. During their time in disguise, the CEO carefully observes employees' skills and attitudes, later revealing their identity to reward those who excel.

I had a preconceived notion that virtues such as humanity,

> "
> If you are wearing red-colored glasses
> by your stereotypes, preconceptions, and biases,
> you are going to see red all over the place,
> no matter how blue the world is.
> "

cooperation, compassion, empathy, caring, and sacrifice would be difficult to embrace in the rationalistic American ethos. However, the show made me realize that regardless of differences in values or cultural relativity, humans are inherently homogeneous and that interpersonal relationships, integrity and trust, and leading by example positively affect productivity and climate in organizations of all sizes.

For this shared human sentiment to serve as a driving force for organizational growth, it is essential to avoid stereotypes. Preconceived notions about American sentiment, or any other group, do not contribute to positive organizational progress. Managers, in particular, must remain mindful of their significant influence on employees and strive to foster an environment of understanding and inclusivity.

One of the episodes from an old comedy program comes

across in my head. A young man with a mustache was taking a nap. His friend melted down some foul-smelling cheese and smeared it on the young man's mustache to tease the young man. When the foul odor hit his nostrils, the young man woke up with a root face. He moved around the house, desperately trying to find the source of the terrible odor, but when he couldn't, he ran outside in frustration and shouted,

"The whole world is rotten!"

This episode reminds me of some people who, when searching for the source of an unpleasant smell—the cause of their fault— look outward or blame others instead of reflecting on themselves.

We live our lives through notions shaped by our learning and experiences, much like seeing the world through our colored glasses. To truly understand people and situations as they are, we need clear lenses. If you are wearing red-colored glasses shaped by your stereotypes, preconceptions, and biases, you'll see red everywhere, even when the world is truly blue.

You may believe you see the world objectively, but if your mindset has remained unchanged over time, it's worth taking a moment to pause and evaluate your actions. The higher your position in an organization and the more power you hold, the greater the risk of unknowingly viewing people and situations through tinted lenses shaped by your own biases and assumptions.

Therefore, it is important to reflect on your stereotypes in social life. If you recognize any negativity, such as preconceived notions and biases, make an effort to change them. Breaking these mental frames requires shifting your perspective from "me" to "we" and embracing a collaborative mindset as a habit.

Authentic communication and meaningful relationships can only be built when we move in the same direction. The ideal leader in an organization embodies wholeness: they are respectful, attentive, caring, accountable, humble, consistent, and lead by example.

By adopting a clear, unbiased perspective and embracing the core values of humanity in our interactions with employees, we create an environment where individuals can thrive, and organizations can flourish.

Work Life and Satisfaction

Are those office workers happier than that old couple?

"Are you happy with your work life?"

If you were to pose this question to an office worker, what kind of answer would you expect? "Satisfaction" is a highly subjective concept, often varying greatly from person to person. I would define it as "a state of mind where one's metaphysical or physical desires are fulfilled beyond expectations." From this perspective, satisfaction can be seen as a self-assessment of a particular situation, shaped by one's desires and how well they feel those desires have been met.

Anyone who works for any length of time would know that the work life is simple and monotonous. A repetition of rushing from work to work with the occasional coworker hangout for camaraderie and a weekend of relaxation to rejuvenate the body and mind in preparation for next week's work.

Judging by appearances, not just work life but life itself often seems monotonous. Many of us battle the "Monday blues," waking up each day feeling uninspired and unmotivated. We drag our weary bodies to work, burdened as if carrying the weight of our entire family. Then, with furrowed brows of irritation and fatigue, we struggle to complete our tasks, counting down the hours until it's time to leave.

Nonetheless, a significant number of employees come to work with their dreams, excited by the challenge, and look forward to tomorrow with reward and hope despite the physically and mentally demanding working conditions.

Everyone encounters uncomfortable or challenging situations at work, both professionally and interpersonally. These can include criticism and reprimands from bosses, gossip and backstabbing from coworkers, departmental conflicts and arguments, and other unforeseen issues that are often difficult to navigate. In such situations, employees with negative personality traits are more likely to feel depressed, frustrated, and perpetually stressed.

In Korea, it's still common to meet up with a close friend or acquaintance for a drink to vent frustrations. However, in the U.S., even if you have close friends, meeting them without prior arrangements is difficult due to time and distance constraints. Moreover, arranging transportation late at night after drinking—whether a ride or taxi—adds another layer of inconvenience.

For these reasons, even when faced with difficult situations at work, we often need to bottle up our frustrations and go home feeling lonely and isolated. When we return home, we may want to vent to our families, but often hold back, fearing it might add to their worries.

A typical workday involves planning, meetings, agreements, decisions, execution, and evaluation. Depending on your position and role, you might also take on additional, less visible but crucial responsibilities, such as managing functional teams or directing the workforce. We all aspire to perform meaningful work, yet at times, we must tackle tasks that feel unnecessary.

This can lead to negative emotions such as anger, frustration, and impatience, especially when mistakes or failures occur. Conversely, positive emotions like fulfillment, hope, and gratitude arise when our good performance, accomplishments, and attitude are acknowledged through promotions and bonuses.

Do those people look happy?

People quit work for a variety of reasons. Over the years, I have had the opportunity to conduct exit interviews with employees who decided to leave. Through these conversations, I have gathered various insights into their reasons for departure. Below is a brief summary of some of the most common responses.

"There is no vision for the company," "I was not treated with respect as an individual," "My boss and the company's executives lack leadership," "I worked hard to the best of my ability and was not compensated fairly," "It is difficult to focus on my work in a heavy organizational atmosphere with no communication," and "In many ways, this is not a company I would recommend to anyone I know," etc.

Based on the reasons described, it seems that some employees in organizations are perpetually contemplating leaving. However, it is rarely the case that the fault lies solely with either the company or the employee. Even when an arbitration process is in place to address issues, some employees tend to justify their actions and beliefs rather than reflect or adapt. Hypocritical double standards continue to persist in organizations. Furthermore, these subjective thoughts and personal narratives often spread to other employees and even to the outside world through gossip and backstabbing.

Finding the ideal environment, company, or person in life is

> "
> When you have a clear vision of the future,
> you need to have a clear sense of purpose, strong willpower,
> and a sense of urgency and desperation before you set goals and plans.
> "

rare, and even if you do, you're likely to find something flaws.

Therefore, rather than seeking an ideal world externally, I believe that it would be wiser to explore and fulfill your aspirations within your inner self. In that vein, being an employee of any organization requires cultivating an attitude that embraces enjoyment and seeks fulfillment in the work whenever possible.

In reality, we occasionally and unexpectedly experience contentment, peace, and even happiness as we strive day by day to find positive meaning in our lives and work. The great and ideal future we vaguely anticipate is seldom, if ever, readily within reach.

Therefore, if you aspire to a specific vision for your future, you must cultivate a clear sense of purpose, unwavering willpower, a sense of urgency, and even a touch of desperation. This foundation allows you to set specific goals, devise actionable plans, and address any readiness issues. At this stage, it is crucial to take a candid inventory of your knowledge, skills, and attitudes, being honest about where you currently stand. As we journey from where we are to where we aspire to be, it is essential to develop the habit of persistence, even when the path is challenging or painful. One critical aspect to remember is the value of time. Whether in our personal lives or work, time is our most finite and precious resource, and we must prioritize it above all else.

One late afternoon in early fall, I observed a large group of office workers walking up and down Park Avenue in Manhattan, New York City. Dressed in suits, they were bustling about without a sideways glance. They walked two or three times faster than the usual pace of typical tourists, displaying various facial expressions. Some appeared cheerful, others serious, while some showed no emotion.

Then I noticed an elderly couple dressed as tourists strolling between the office workers, and a thought struck me like a flash of light:

"Are those office workers happier than that old couple?"

As I watch the people passing by, I couldn't help but think how transformative it would be if everyone embraced the idea that our mindset shapes our reality. Even in challenging personal and professional situations, we hold the power to find comfort, and, like carefree travelers, embrace laughter and joy. Ultimately, it all depends on how we choose to perceive the world around us.

Five Core Values for Communication and Relationships

Respect, Honesty, Trust, Attention and Care, Family-Like

Your coworkers form social connections that cannot replicate the comfort and intimacy of family relationships. As a result, having deep conversations with them may not come easily. However, the total time spent with coworkers is often much greater and involves more complex interactions than the time spent with family.

Each coworker has their own values, personality, habits, and background, yet they work together toward a common goal within the same environment of the company. Work-life is a harmony of heterogeneity and homogeneity. To use a food analogy, we have the concept of a salad, where each vegetable brings out its flavor, and the concept of a soup, where the flavors of different ingredients blend.

Therefore, it is a significant challenge to bring together people with different values, personalities, habits, and backgrounds. In the United States, this challenge is further amplified by the diversity of races, cultures, and languages. Achieving harmony and pursuing a common goal requires significant recognition and effort. In the complex dynamics of organizational behavior, maintaining communication, fostering positive relationships, and making work both enjoyable and fulfilling present ongoing challenges.

Throughout my extensive career in American organizations, I have focused on uniting diverse individuals toward a shared goal. To achieve this, I have employed the following methods:

It involves consistently and repeatedly communicating and supporting diverse employees and aligning with a shared goal.

From that perspective, I repeatedly shared with my direct reports five core values for communication and relationships: respect, honesty, trust, attention and care, and family, in that order.

First and foremost, the importance of respect cannot be overstated. When members of an organization are not yet familiar with each other, they often rely on profile elements such as skills, education, competencies, experience, specialties, majors, or even age to establish their positioning within the group. This is akin to how, in Tae Kwon Do, one can gauge an opponent's skill level simply observing their sparring stance. However, before we focus on these external profile attributes, it is crucial to prioritize mutual respect for one another as fellow social beings.

Many people prioritize their outward image over their

true character. They pay closer attention to and place more importance on the company's reputation and/or the job title on a business card rather than on the person behind them. Unfortunately, we often judge others using these superficial metrics, categorizing and ranking positions as "higher" or "lower" based on such evaluation.

However, as human beings, we are all equal and deserving of mutual respect—a fundamental human virtue. Respect should transcend factors such as ability, education, competence, experience, talent, specialty, major, age, gender, wealth, or reputation. By respecting others as equal human beings, we uphold basic courtesy, allowing us to genuinely focus on and connect with one another.

Once an environment of mutual respect is in place, the next step is to realize an honest relationship. Intentional and deceitful lies, thoughtless actions devoid of genuine emotion or impact, and superficial lip service fail to connect with others. Instead, they hurt and alienate people. Honest communication, on the other hand, builds genuine relationships. It creates a foundation for sincere exchanges where true feelings and thoughts can be openly shared, strengthening mutual trust and understanding.

When relationships are built on respect and honesty, trust naturally follows. Having coworkers you can rely on fosters a

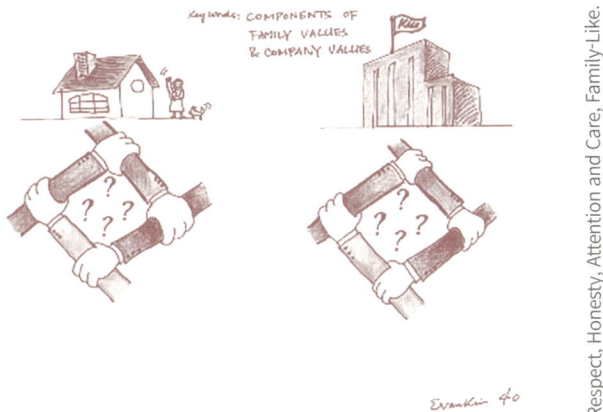

positive and supportive work environment.

While salary, title, and rewards are important to employees, having trusted colleagues is equally significant. Since a substantial portion of time is spent at the workplace, cultivating close and dependable relationships with coworkers is essential. If these relationships are instead characterized by distrust and suspicion, the workplace becomes a breeding ground for discomfort, frustration, anger, and resentment. Over time, this negativity can undermine morale and severely harm productivity.

However, in relationships built on trust, mistakes and shortcomings can be understood. Of course, this understanding is within bounds on common sense, and while ethical and legal principles are upheld, mutual respect and a positive, inclusive attitude strengthen the relationship.

These relationships can foster a sense of psychological belonging and stability among team members and, on a large scale, within the organization. When trust is established, we naturally become more interested in and attentive to the other person, creating a spirit of sharing and mutual support.

This shift replaces a self-centered mindset focused solely on personal gain or loss with an environment where empathy and tolerance take precedence. Such a transformation not only strengthens individual connections but also contributes to a healthier and more collaborative organizational culture.

Generally, organizations are structured and task-oriented, making it challenging to foster an atmosphere of care or attention. However, incorporating even a small amount of care and attentiveness into interactions can significantly enhance the overall atmosphere and strengthen relationships within the organization and team.

By fostering a culture of mutual support and empathy, the workplace becomes more collaborative and enjoyable for everyone involved.

For example, if you notice a coworker's depressed mood and take a time to engage with them in a meaningful conversation or write them a thoughtful letter, it can make a significant impact. Remembering a junior employee's difficult situation and quietly help them at the right time, or touch their feelings or wounds

> "For your social and organizational life, show Respect and Honesty. Then, earn Trust with Attention and Care, we become Family-like."

with attention and care, you can build a solid relationship.

In this way, by fostering respect, honesty, trust, attention and care, your organization can transform into a second family, like members of household who share meals together, allowing for strong and lasting relationships. The final value, "family or family-like," emerges naturally when the other four values are practiced with sincerity. This familial bond, built on shared understanding and compassion, fosters stronger and more lasting connections. When visualizing this family-like atmosphere, concepts such as love and sacrifice often come to mind. While these virtues are traditionally associated with family relationships, extending them to coworkers can be challenging but not impossible. Though rare, such bonds can develop within a workplace.

If you strip away pretenses, genuinely show up for others, and practice these core values above, you will find yourself on the path to effective communication and meaningful relationships that enhance both personal and organizational well-being.

Why Eat Together?

Let's meet up for a meal someday!

In social life, one of the most widely accepted ways to communicate and build positive relationships is over a meal, so we often use the phrase "Let's grab a meal!" In Korean corporate life, it is also a way to build rapport for unity.

Regardless of wealth, power, or ability, humans eat to stay alive. Throughout history, countless wars have been fought for ideological, religious, and political reasons, the most practical reason being to gain more territory and resources to provide food and shelter for their people.

The five human desires are food, sleep, fame, money, and sex. Among those, food, along with sleep, is a fundamental human need that lasts as long as we live. Therefore, it's important that we maintain a good diet. If we can enjoy good food in a relaxed atmosphere, surrounded by people we appreciate and engaging conversation, it brings a sense of great satisfaction. This holistic experience nurtures us physically, mentally, and emotionally, contributing to our overall well-being.

On a social and organizational level, the meal is much more than a means of metabolism and human indulgence. Whenever a country's supreme ruler travels to another country, a state dinner is a symbolic event. As such, meals remain the ultimate social gathering across time, countries, cultures, and races.

Whether it is with family, friends, coworkers, or acquaintances, the process and approach to sharing meals, dinners, or banquets often vary based on the goals and objectives. So why do we gather to eat together in our social lives?

First, because meals provide an effective platform for socializing. We have a physiological phenomenon called "we eat to live," so we share meals and feel a sense of unity and togetherness while eating the same or similar foods.

It is the same idea as taking a sauna together, where you get to know each other on a more intimate level. Similar to sauna, eating can be seen as a process of shedding barriers and opening up to one another, making it something we typically do with people we seek comfort and intimacy with.

Generally, you would not voluntarily eat with someone you do not like. Of course, a meal with a clear intention or purpose can happen whether you like it or not.

Second, meals are used as an occasion or opportunity for

communication. During mealtime, you can expect discussions of topics that were previously difficult to address and reestablishment of long-estranged relationships. This time also allows for breakthroughs in communication, fostering mutual understanding, consultation, and bonding.

Meals are often accompanied by liquor. When consumed in moderation, it can create a positive atmosphere by serving as a social lubricant, transforming a formal setting into a warm and emotionally engaging one. However, you should always be aware of the side effects of liquor.

Third, food is also a tool for fostering a sense of belonging. Despite our differences in nationality, race, gender, culture,

Let's meet up for a meal someday!

ability, wealth, education, and other social conditions—which often lead to hierarchical structures—all humans are equal in intrinsic value. However, it's unfortunate and undesirable that such discrimination still exists, often unnoticed.

Eating together is a symbolic message of putting aside some of the social conditions and hierarchy, eating "one pot meal," and acting like a Korean family. Family members in Chinese characters symbolize the "食" meal and "口" mouth, so social acquaintances and coworkers who can eat together are like another family in a positive sense. However, be careful not to let this symbolism become a divisive factor.

Fourth, meals are also used for political, strategic, social, and ostentatious purposes: these are rituals to assert one's social status as a wealthy person, a high-ranking person, an employer, or a celebrity, and to receive corresponding recognition and treatment.

It establishes order and hierarchy among participants, acts as a rite of passage to affirm leadership and loyalty, and implicitly realigns the "contractor" and "subcontractor" when necessary. It also serves marketing purposes to solidify the organization.

When we talk about meals, we also think about company dinners. Company dinners have significant cultural differences depending on the company's tone, especially for Korean-

> Meals are a central part of our social and professional lives, and they can lead to better communication, stronger relationships, and more cohesion.

American companies in the U.S. The culture varies depending on the CEO's personality and the ethnicity and age distribution of the workforce.

Therefore, to have a productive dinner at a Korean-American company in the U.S., executives and meeting organizers need to listen to the voices of American, young, and female employees in particular and be mindful of the following areas where employees are uncomfortable and reluctant to participate.

Announcing schedules abruptly and without input from employees, forcing participation as an extension of work, making employees feel uncomfortable and anxious if they don't attend, requiring time and effort outside of work to prepare for the event, following a cookie-cutter format for speeches and pep talks by management, and focusing on work during the event. Hierarchical and rigid situations, unnecessary and inappropriate interference in personal life and advice, slandering bosses or coworkers over drinks, not letting you leave halfway through, complaining about the company or work, verbal abuse, sexual harassment, forcing you to drink...

Meals are a central part of our social and professional lives, and they can lead to better communication, stronger relationships, and more cohesion. However, meals and dinners do not always have positive outcomes, and you need to be careful to avoid negative consequences in some situations.

Meals play an important role in both our personal and professional lives. Can you immediately think of someone who might casually invite you to grab a meal? And at the same time, are there people you would consider inviting for a meal? While social connections are valuable, it is ideal to be in a position where you can comfortably accept invitations from many and, in turn, extend invitations to others.

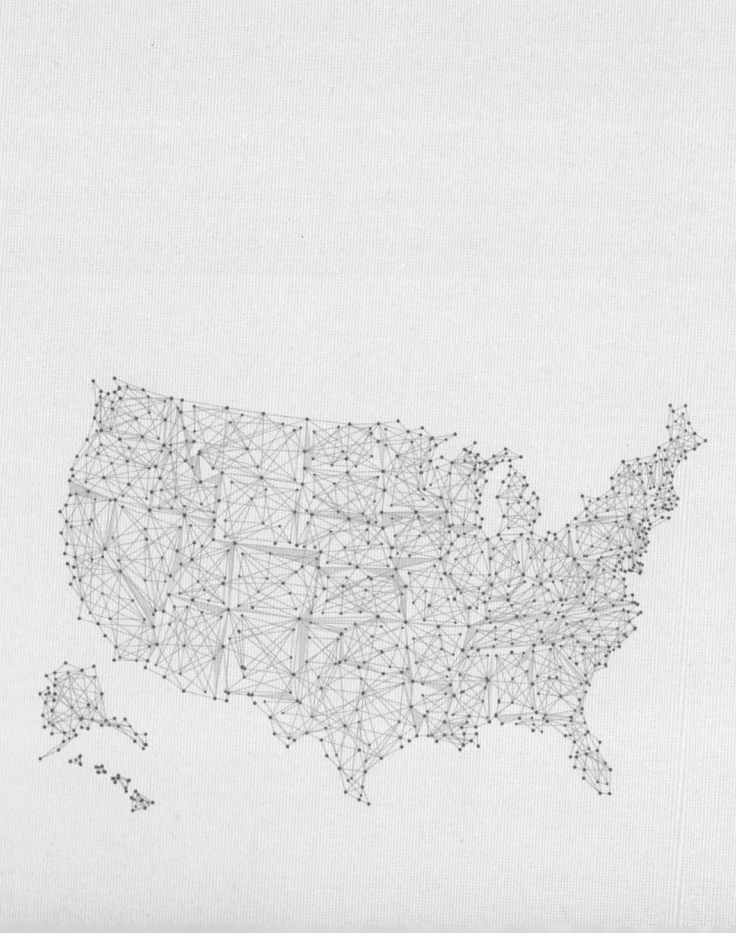

American Organization

"STAND" Makes Leader 101 a Reality

Personal Management Innovation

How do we survive going forward?

Do you remember "Sears" department store chain in U.S.?

"Sears", founded in Chicago in 1892, was the largest retailer in the U.S. Hundreds of pages of colorful catalogs were published every year, and I remember ogling the various products within them. Years ago, I even went to Sears to buy a smart TV, but Sears fell on hard times and filed for bankruptcy in 2018. Since then, "Sears" has been liquidating most of its stores and winding down the business, with only a dozen or so remaining in the U.S. and Puerto Rico as of June 2023.

It is not only Sears, but we are seeing blue-chip companies like Kodak, Xerox, Motorola, and others, which have been at the forefront for more than 100 years, fade into history in the blink of an eye.

We are in the midst of the 4th industrial revolution, a period of profound digital transformation. The Internet of Things, DNA recombination, robotization, artificial intelligence, virtual reality, augmented reality, metaverses, and more are transforming the world at a frightening pace, forcing us to learn and adapt.

As such, I cannot help but think about how the world will change in the future and how humans will need to respond. From that perspective, I think I call this the "VUCA" era; volatile, uncertain, complex, and ambiguous.

Amazon was founded in 1994. It became an e-commerce platform for buying and selling a wide variety of goods, including the creation, sale, and distribution of e-books, which were different from traditional paper books. Today, Amazon is pioneering many future businesses, and it took less than 30 years to get here.

Now, when I need to purchase something, I open the Amazon application on my smartphone. From checking out the products to finalizing my order, it takes just enough time for a cup of coffee, and I enjoy the convenience and speed of having the item I want at my doorstep in a day or two.

In such a situation, what is the future for companies and their employees who continue to operate traditionally and focus on their own style and way of doing things?

Unlike brick-and-mortar commerce, where goods are bought and sold in person, today's producers, suppliers, and consumers operate through online platforms. These platforms, supported by various applications, have evolved into seamless, interactive, and comprehensive business models.

Then, COVID-19 struck in 2020, causing a pandemic, and our once highly developed civilization was brought to a screeching halt by a tiny virus. It also reshaped the culture and customs of social life: work from home, virtual meetings, social distancing, and contactless delivery.

Add to this the 4th industrial revolution, the unique mindset of the MZ generation, and evolving culture and customs of social life, and the time has come to consider new ways of survival. Perhaps it is time to think about "how to survive in the future" rather than "how to live in the future."

The key word in all of the above is "change." Throughout history, civilizations, races, nations, and more have risen and fallen. Businesses are no exception, and there are countless examples of blue-chip companies that seemed very strong in the modern era but did not survive. The main reason they could not survive was that there was no change, and they became complacent. Past glory is no guarantee of the future.

We often use the phrase management innovation as "re-engineering." The term gained popularity in the 1980s in business circles to describe a revolutionary change in management practices. As defined by management scholar

Michael Martin Hammer, it is "the fundamental rethinking and radical redesign of business processes to dramatically improve and reinvent key indicators of business performance, such as cost, quality, service, and speed. Again, the emphasis is on radical change.

The importance of change can be traced back to biologist Charles Robert Darwin's theory of survival of the fittest. As is widely known, survival of the fittest means that only those organisms that adapt to changes in their environment will survive, while those that do not will die out and disappear.

When applied to organizations, this can be interpreted as: "To fully respond to changes in the business environment and achieve relent growth, continuous adaptation is necessary."

This idea can be further refined through the 3Cs: Customer, Change, and Competitiveness. Companies exist to satisfy their customers and the markets they operate in. To do so, they must continuously and innovatively adapt to changes in the business environment, and secure the competitiveness needed to survive and thrive in a competitive landscape.

Change is an integral part of business transformation both conceptually and practically and it is not limited to civilizations, races, nations, and companies. This principle applies to individuals as well.

Although there is some variation among countries, the distribution of gross domestic product (GDP) generally shows the government at the top, with most businesses in the middle. The foundation that supports both the government and businesses is the labor force.

In this context, a highly skilled workforce is valued and rewarded with significant responsibility, authority, and compensation for consistently delivering results for governments, companies, and other profit organizations. As a result, most people aspire to be key players in their societies and organizations.

To achieve this, they must proactively adapt to the rapid changes in the world. Without the necessary abilities, knowledge,

> Change is an integral part of business transformation and it is not limited to civilizations, races, nations, and companies. It is also true for individuals.

skills, and attitudes, it becomes difficult to thrive in today's fast-faced environment. Recognizing this, individuals must urgently work to develop these qualities to successfully navigate and respond to global shifts.

Nowadays, artificial intelligence, big data, the Internet of Things, robots, drones, autonomous driving, and other terms that represent technological change have become essential parts of our everyday vocabulary. So, people with the relevant abilities, knowledge, skills, and attitudes are highly sought after.

As we live in such a world, personal transformation for survival and development must be implemented immediately. We should design a clear blueprint for life and work with purpose and goals based on the 5W1H (Who, What, When, Where, Why, How) principle and then create specific detailed plans with solid aspirations. Being recognized as talented by society and within our organization marks the first step toward personal and professional innovation.

I have spent my life creating a blueprint for living and working for change, and I remember one of my resolutions from decades ago that I take to heart and am still working on.

"I will dedicate my life to ensuring that my family always keeps their smiles and that their hearts stay strong and healthy. I will fulfill this responsibility with unwavering devotion. I will also do my best to support my children in living rich and fulfilling lives, both mentally and emotionally.

My Between Words and Actions

Winners prove their words with their actions

I remember an executive from an organization I worked for a long time ago who was highly admired for his skills, experience, and education. In meetings and conversations, he was always logical and flawless in his arguments. His knowledge spanned across business, politics, sociology, history, philosophy, and more, when critiquing and commenting, he resembled a consultant. He also had a certain innocence when introducing himself and displayed humility when sharing his opinions.

However, one day, I unintentionally discovered that he had been engaging in behaviors that violated his morals and ethics. In that moment, the positive image I had of him shattered, leaving me deeply disappointed by his duplicity.

He was constantly charging his expenses to the company and often took company supplies home with him. He also littered, spat in the sink, and displayed other misbehavior whenever no one was watching or around.

The word meaning "refrain from doing anything that goes against mortality when being alone (慎獨)" appears in both "The Great Learning (大學)" and "The Doctrine of The Mean (中庸)" in "The Four Books" in China. The idea is that self-improvement comes from avoiding wrong actions when you are alone, not from seeking others' approval. This executive seems to have practiced this backward.

Houston, Texas, is home to the Lakewood Church. It is a very large church. Joel Osteen, the pastor, delivers sermons not only to his congregation but also through TV and radio. I sometimes listen to his sermons in the car on my way home from work, and a particular sticks out in my head.

Winners prove their words with their actions.

It was a particularly windy Saturday afternoon. After returning to church from errands and parking his car, Pastor Joel Austin got out of his car and opened the backseat door to grab his briefcase. At that moment, the newspapers he had placed on top of his briefcase were blown away by the wind and scattered in all directions.

At the time, there were only a few cars parked in the large parking lot, no one else was around, and there was a church member for cleaning up anyway, so he figured he could get away with it. But at the same time, he had these thoughts.

"Joel, you are the pastor of this church, and you are to lead by example, whether anyone is there or not."

After a moment's hesitation, he began to run here and there, picking up the scattered newspapers and gathering them up. The wind was still whipping around, so the newspapers kept flying around instead of staying in place, so he chased them from place to place.

After a while, he gathered up all the newspapers and was walking back to his car when he felt a strange sensation and turned his head to see someone waving at him from some distance away. As he got closer, he realized it was a couple from the church he knew, and they were watching the whole thing.

"We were going to make a bet on whether you would pick up the newspapers. Of course, the bet did not work out because we were on the same side, and we were so happy to see you pick them up, as we expected."

At that moment, a cold sweat broke out on Pastor Joel Austin's back.

What would have happened if he had not picked up the newspaper and just walked into the church?

The old saints often stressed the importance of consistency in one's speech, while also emphasizing the need to take responsibility for the words spoken. Once words are out of our mouths, they are impossible to take back, no matter how much we want to pick them up.

Despite knowing this, we often go with the flow of our thoughts and feelings, usually making mistakes and regretting them; we say things we do not mean to get through the moment, agree others to maintain relationships even if it conflicts with our values, and make promises we cannot keep to impress or show off.

In social and professional life, words are not only a key means of communication and interaction but also a major indicator of a person's character. We can get to know someone to a certain extent by the content and quality of their speech.

Words are special and are tied up in knots with actions. When your words and actions match, your credibility and trustworthiness increase. The key to aligning words and actions is sincerity. Words that come from a sincere heart almost always lead to trustworthy behavior. We know this because we have experienced it firsthand.

> "A Talmudic proverb says, "Losers excuse their actions by their words, and winners prove their words by their actions."
> We must apply this to ourselves."

The phrase "what's on the outside is what's on the inside" means that your words and actions match. The reason we have two ears and one mouth seems to be a message from God to listen carefully to what others say and be careful what you say, which can also be interpreted as listening twice as carefully and speaking only once. In reality, serious individuals may not speak much, but the depth of their sincerity is evident in the few words and sentences they do express.

A Talmudic proverb says, "Losers excuse their actions by their words, and winners prove their words by their actions." We should reflect on this by substituting "loser" with "fool" and "winner" with "wise." As I navigate my roles within my personal life, family, and society, I must ask myself: Am I a fool or a wise person?

We feel dignity with those who are heavy-handed and think those who are light are the tricker. Because of this view, individuals who have significant influence over the public, including politicians, are expected to behave in a more exemplary manner. Religious figures, in particular, must embed behavior and attitudes that inspire respect and admiration in their sense of mission to lead people in the right direction.

However, history has shown that wherever power and profit are concentrated, immoral and unethical behavior often follows, including within religious institutions. The media frequently portrays religious organizations with power comparable to large corporations, religious leaders wielding influence over CEOs, and politically driven figures who manipulate their followers through lies, incitement, and slander. We can only hope that the misdeeds of these misguided religious figures do not cast a negative shadow on the broader community.

When your thoughts are organized in your head, it is easier to speak logically. Wisdom, knowledge, and information can be conveyed through words in an intelligent, rational, and realistic way.

However, if you are solely on your thoughts to express your intentions, you cannot fully convey your feelings and emotions. Your words must also be infused with your heart. The heart is the seat of emotions and feelings, capable of expressing both positive sentiments like joy, happiness, care, and acceptance, as well as negative ones like sadness, frustration, anger, and hatred. Regardless of your emotional state, when you express your feelings honestly, your words carry more weight because they are genuine.

We often refer to the Chinese character for faith (信), which combines the characters for people (人) and words (言), meaning "people's words," This can be interpreted as "when people's words are true and trustworthy; we give and receive faith."

If words reflect their thoughts and feelings, then belief is the value that is imprinted on others when their thoughts and feelings are right. Right thoughts and hearts can be proven when they are followed by sincere actions. Even if the words are slurred, faith is bound to sprout if they are followed by sincere actions. From that point of view, I think that sincere actions by leading by example are much more important than a hundred words.

Words and actions should be aligned, clear, and meaningful. We must see them as one, for they are the promises we make to ourselves and others.

Diagnostic Technique for Leaders

The manager does not know what he does not know

In the company, there are employees who perform tasks out of habit, relying on experience and routine inertia. They consider themselves competent and frequently evaluate and criticize others as well.

This is the case of blindness (目不見睫) in the organization. In Chinese, there is a proverbial saying that the eye cannot see the eyebrow, meaning that it is easy to see the faults in others but not in yourself. In English word, "The pot calls the kettle black."

For a successful work life, it is necessary to move beyond self-centered thinking and adopt an attitude of respect toward others. Especially as a manager, it is important to be objective and rational when receiving advice and counsel about yourself. In this article, I would like to share some examples of how you can diagnose managers and employees from this perspective.

The following are types of managers. You can ask people in your organization which one represents the worst case.

① The manager knows what he knows.
② The manager knows what he doesn't know.
③ The manager doesn't know what he knows.
④ The manager doesn't know what he doesn't know.

Note that "what" refers to a specific manager's strengths, weaknesses, competencies, personality, attitudes, and so on. "knows" and "doesn't know" refer to "recognizing or acknowledging," or "not recognizing or not acknowledging."

Types ① and ② are managers who have first reflected, analyzed and evaluated themselves. Because they recognize or acknowledge their level, they can distinguish the good from the bad in their behavior, so they are more likely to improve their shortcomings through self-management in the future.

Type ③ are managers who are less concerned with themselves and less thoughtful. They tend to be less challenged professionally and take interpersonal relationships lightly.

Type ④, on the other hand, refers to managers who are person of concern. They might act out of arrogance and complacency, thinking, "I don't really need to know" or "It's fine even if I don't know." If this attitude becomes a habit, it can turn them into self-centered managers who dominate their employees with a sense of superiority.

Here is a representative look at three middle managers I observed in practice.

The first, a middle manager called "K," had a tremendous amount of pride and confidence in the work she was doing-she was excited to do work that she thought she was good at and that she loved, regardless of the needs of the company or how important it was. But K's ego-driven approach to her work resulted in jumbled priorities and poor time management. This imbalance of time and effort often negatively impacted on other important tasks. Her coworkers tried to help her prioritize and manage her time, but she would react emotionally, leading to a negative atmosphere in the organization.

Second, a junior manager named "L" was asked by her department head to report back with a short list of appropriate gifts for a company event and a price range. The department head thought it would take only two to three hours. However, contrary to his expectations, L spent far more time than necessary, searching websites all day, including time spent by her junior staff. As a result, all of her more prioritized tasks were postponed. When the department head pointed this out

The manager does not know what he does not know.

to her, L felt unappreciated, claiming that her efforts were not recognized.

The takeaway from K and L's story is important. In practice, assessing employees' contribution to a task requires a combination of their competencies, including their knowledge and experience of the task, their understanding of the importance, urgency, and difficulty of the task, and their ability to manage the task objectively and rationally. Ideally, they should achieve 100% or more of the task, but even 80% is acceptable. Therefore, a principle that you must adhere to in your work is to prioritize the most important things and leave the less prioritized things behind because wasted time and effort due to misplaced priorities, as K and L did, is a major cause of low productivity in a company.

To avoid this situation, the task leader should be proactive in discussing the priorities with the task assignees, helping them understand the context, explaining the quantitative evaluation metrics, and setting deadlines.

Third, "P" is a self-directed manager who loves his work and whose investment of time and effort in it is far above that of other managers. Consequently, his sense of ownership of his work is unparalleled. He is so present at work that it's hard to imagine him having a family life. He is also somewhat stubborn and emotional, so the language he chooses to use when communicating with others, and the way he responds, can be quite abrasive and belligerent. P's job involved collaborating with other departments on many projects. Of course, he worked around day and night when collaborating with other departments. However, during the collaboration, he often encountered problems in discussions and agreements with other departments. Whenever he disagreed with other members, he would use emotional and belligerent communication and attitudes instead of logical and rational discussions. As a result, other departments and members

> The line between "working hard" and "working effectively" is affected by the capabilities of the parties involved, but it also depends heavily on the values and communication skills of managers.

avoided working with him.

P was highly competent and exhibited great enthusiasm in his role, but his lack of collaboration resulted in outcomes that did not meet expectations. When I think about P, I think about the advice, "If you want to go fast, go alone; if you want to go far, go together."

The lesson to take away from these examples is the distinction between "working hard" and "working smart." We often hear the phrase "we work hard," so how do we respond to a request to hire more people because we are working hard but cannot seem to keep up? We should keep in mind Parkinson's law, which states that "the number of employees is not directly proportional to the amount of work completed, but rather tends to increase due to psychological factors that lead individuals to fill their available time with additional tasks." This explains why, even with additional hires, the workload per person doesn't decrease, as people naturally fill the time available to them.

When you work, some tasks are highly prioritized, while others may be less important but equally as urgent. The key to getting work done is to organize your scattered tasks into the most efficient process that produces the most effective results. If your time and effort aren't being translated into efficiency and effectiveness, you are just adding to your workload without getting anything done. Sometimes, hard work without results is viewed positively from a loyalty and commitment perspective. This makes those who have delivered results in the pursuit of efficiency and effectiveness feel unappreciated and ignored.

The line between "working hard" and "working smart and effectively" is influenced by the abilities of the individuals involved, but it also depends heavily on the values and communication skills of managers.

As a highly collaborative manager, you need to have a clear understanding of your role and constantly reflect, analyze, and evaluate your work-related skills, experience, strengths, weaknesses, and approaches, depending on the project.

Some managers claim to be doing things for the company's benefit, but in reality, they are doing things based on their interests and preferences. This situation makes it difficult to ultimately contribute to the company's interests.

Managers must also care about their staff and their roles. It's essential to clearly understand their attitudes and behaviors, as well as the specifics of their tasks and how they perform them. By acting on these principles, you can provide appropriate direction and suggestions for improvement, and objective, rational evaluations of their results and performance.

The Age of Lifelong Learning

There's something to learn from anyone, anywhere

We all know that the Fourth Industrial Revolution has begun. The pace of change in the world, driven by technological change, is lightning-fast. With new knowledge, information, vocabulary, and more increasing every day, it can sometimes feel like a burden to try to make sense of it all.

However, the youth of MZ (Millennials & Gen Z) are embracing these changes as a way of life. MZ are sensitive and comfortable with technological change, especially since they are digital natives living in a digital environment since birth. The use of the internet, mobile, artificial intelligence, etc., has become routine, and they are living a basic lifestyle that emphasizes self-improvement and personal investment, horizontal relationships, and respect for individuality. In Korea, we have a term called "소확행 (sohwakhaeng)," which translates to "small but sure happiness." Similarly, new term like "YOLO (You Only Live Once)" have emerged, shaping a new social and cultural identity distinct from previous generations by connecting with contemporary politics, economics, society, and technology.

How do the MZ generation define their parents' generation, including the baby boomers?

Baby boomers like me were taught and practiced to work hard, save, and make sacrifices for the good of society to grow our country's economy and secure our families' finances. I'm concerned that MZ generation see these values as frustratingly outdated and irrelevant, rather than understanding the sacrifices that we made to build a better future.

As we have seen over the generations, the world is ever-changing, and new cultures are created. We adapt to that environment, pursuing and challenging our values, collaborating, and competing with others.

In an era where change is the norm, learning is essential to maximizing your value. To grow and meet the demands of your time and environment, you must stay engaged with the world and make self-directed learning a lifelong habit.

It reminds me of how eagles raise their eaglets. Eagles build nests in cliffs to raise eaglets. When eaglets are young, eagles soften the nest with grass and fur and put food in eaglet mouths. But as the eaglets get older, the nest becomes uncomfortable, and they remove the grass and fur. So the eagle encourages eaglets to be active and flap their wings outside the nest. At the same time, the eagle leaves food in the nest, so that if the stronger eaglet monopolizes the food, they do not help the weaker one, even if the weaker eaglet is pinched to a bloody pulp by the stronger one's beak. When the eaglets get older, they drop them off a cliff, as they are known to do. The fledglings are clumsy on their wings and soon fall to their deaths. The eagle will catch the eaglets after they have fallen a certain distance and bring them back to the nest. Through repetition of this action, the eaglets learn to flap their wings and eventually learn to fly on their own.

A lesson from the eagle is no small matter. To survive in the jungle of society, where challenges and crises are ever-present, we must take action and adapt.

There's something to learn from anyone, anywhere.

The activity of learning in a society or organization is similar to the idea of building muscles. There are more than 600 muscles in the human body, each with its unique role in human activities such as breathing, circulation, eating, and exercising, etc.

We all know that with consistent strength training, we can transform ourselves into a muscular, handsome physique, or what we call a "toned six-pack body." But if you do not continue strength training, the shape will fade away. Furthermore, developing only certain muscles does not equate to overall health, nor does it mean you are good at all physical activities.

A similar phenomenon can be found at work. In addition to work-related knowledge and skills, employees also need interpersonal competencies such as communication, leadership, and caring. These competencies are difficult to quantify because they are highly personal and subjective, involving psychology, emotions, and sensitivity, so they can only be learned through experience and not theory alone.

To thrive in society or an organization, we must cultivate both the specialized knowledge and skills, as well as the broader interpersonal abilities needed to succeed.

Strength training takes effort and time, and it also involves pain and injury, but if you are willing to put in the time and effort, coupled with a lifelong passion and commitment to

> "
> In an era where change is the norm,
> learning is essential to maximizing your value.
> "

learning, you will grow the muscles of knowledge, skills, and other competencies that will enable you to function successfully in society and organizations.

There is a phrase in Chinese, "眼下無人," which means "no one is under one's eyes." It describes an arrogant person who looks down on others and is full of oneself. They are characterized by self-centeredness, and their heads are full of money, power, honor, and prestige, as a result, they live by "pretending"— pretending to be good, to know everything, to have it all together. And because they believe in their stereotypes, they often do not embrace the changing world—technology, life, culture, rituals, etc.

In organizational management, such individuals are particularly dangerous. Often, it is the arrogant manager, rather than the incompetent team members, who has the most damaging effect on the organizational climate. Arrogant managers, rightly or wrongly, are stubbornly self-assertive; their arrogance makes them slow to improve themselves, and they have a hard time connecting with colleagues because they interact with them based on prejudice rather than genuine conviction. Not surprisingly, employees shun them.

The world is a learning ground if you have a clear purpose and reason for learning and a forward-thinking attitude and demeanor with integrity, diligence, and humility. There is so much to learn from nature in the sky, mountains, and oceans, as well as from life in animals, plants, and insects.

True leaders approach learning differently. They make reading a habit, consistently take notes on what they learn, and respect the ideas and actions of others, regardless of their status.

On the other hand, bosses have nowhere else to look but down, looking at people because they want to be at the top. They are full of arrogance as if they deserve to be at the top. There is no willingness or effort to learn from them.

What, then, motivates learning in social life? There are two key drivers: The first is the desire for competitive advantage fueled by self-esteem and passion; the second is the pursuit of self-improvement driven by authenticity and humility.

Many of the great monks make ardent effort or exertion, enthusiastic practice, or rigorous self-discipline and have retreat periods in the Buddhist in summer and winter or meditation until the moment they take their last breath and constantly pursue learning. They strive to master their disciplines, realize their wisdom, and enlighten the world with their lives.

Deep waters run silent, much like how we achieve self-actualization by filling our hearts to the brim. In this process, pride, competitiveness, and envy disappear, and a calm, relaxed, generous, resolute, and clear mind emerges. I hope to continue the practice of emptying myself by imitating those who truly practice learning.

The Difference Between a Pro and an Amateur

Learn from the rabbit and the tortoise

On weekends, many sports are on TV: basketball, baseball, American football, golf, ice hockey, soccer, and more. In between these sports broadcasts, big-name companies take advantage of the breaks to run a variety of marketing campaigns and showcase their exciting commercials. Currently, the most expensive commercial airtime per second in the United States is during the "Super Bowl," the championship game of American football. When leading companies in various industries debut their new commercials, viewers enjoy both the excitement of the game and the creativity of the advertising. In recent years, Korean companies have joined the ranks of these advertisers, expanding their influence.

Many sports broadcasts now take place in prime time. Moreover, the substantial marketing investment in a sporting event like the "Super Bowl" highlights the immense value of the program. When the "Super Bowl" begins, where a scalp ticket costs thousands of dollars or more, roads and streets across the United States become sound still.

Instead, restaurants and sports bars are packed, and families and friends gather at home to watch the game together. It is also the biggest day of the year for potato chips, pizza and beer sales.

One reason so many of us are so passionate about sports is the dedication of the professional athletes who pour themselves into the game, captivating and inspiring us with their performances. Naturally, some amateur athletes also rise to prominence, making their mark in high school or college.

The reality is that while professionals and amateurs may differ in skill, the gap between them can often be quite narrow.

Which one are you?

However, the disparity in attention and salary between professionals and amateurs is immense, driven by the allure of the professional world.

Above all, the lives of professional athletes often resemble unscripted soap operas. It is the soap opera that captures the imagination of the viewers and leaves them on the edge of their seats. Unexpected twists and turns and improbable situations are realized, and viewers are thrilled and vicariously satisfied.

As a result, professional athletes in the U.S. are the equivalent of celebrities and role models for many young people. Along with their fame, they also model for advertisements, earning astronomical amounts of money.

The difference between a pro and an amateur can be summarized in a few ways.

First, there is the difference in income. Compared to amateurs, professionals earn significantly more in many ways.

Second, the difference in level. Even the most talented amateurs rarely make it to the professional ranks. The professional world is reserved for the best—those enter, compete, and survive. Even top performers are cut if they fail to consistently deliver. A pro must maintain peak performance, avoiding injury and inconsistency.

Third, the difference in interest. For amateurs, the school or organization, rather than the individual, is the interest standard. In the professional world, the organization and the individual are the centers of attention.

Someone once defined an amateur as "someone who challenges himself until he reaches his breaking point," and a professional as "someone who shows his worth when he reaches his breaking point." Indeed, we often see professionals who are pushed to their limits in sporting events, miraculously scoring goals to turn the tide in impossible situations where even the most ardent fans have given up.

The distinction between professional and amateur extends far beyond the realm of sports. It permeates all aspects of society, where relentless effort and hard work are essential. High IQ or innate talent alone does not guarantee success.

World-renowned ballerina Kang Soo-Jin, as she was known, woke up every day around 5 in the morning, stretched for more than two hours, and practiced ballet moves for more than 15 hours. In the process, she had to replace more than 250 pairs of toe shoes every season. The scarred and deformed feet she revealed the painstaking work of a ballerina who was supposed to be glamorous and graceful and deeply moved the public.

The late world-renowned conductor and pianist Leonard Bernstein once said, "If I do not practice one day, I know it. If I

> "The difference between a pro and an amateur
> applies equally to all areas of society, with hard work at its core.
> Having a high IQ or being talented cannot guarantee success."

do not practice for two days, my wife and family know it. If I do not practice three days, the audience knows it." His words make us think seriously about what hard work is.

In his book "Outlier," Malcolm Gladwell, a renowned journalist and author, demonstrates that those recognized as the best and most successful in their field have often worked with an intensity and dedication that borders on the extreme, pushing themselves to the very limits.

Three hours a day for ten years adds up to over 10,000 hours. In "Outlier," Gladwell emphasizes that with the level of effort, practice, and focus, you can achieve extraordinary results. However, dedicating three hours a day for ten years while working a full-time job is challenging. Even if you can't commit to the three-hour rule suggested in "Outlier," consistently and persistently working on something regularly can still yield positive results. Do you have something or someone you benchmark against to compete and challenge yourself?

When benchmarking, prioritize specific criteria, field, product, system, etc. that is relevant to you or your company. Choose a benchmark that you have a strong reason to aspire to, and strive to surpass it, aiming to outdo yourself in the process.

The ballerina Soo-Jin Kang did not practice to the point of deforming her toes just because someone told her to. She voluntarily trained herself to exist in the professional world. From that perspective, it's admirable to see someone commit to something for three hours a day for more than a decade.

If you've decided to become a professional at something you believe you're good at, there are some essential ingredients you'll need. First and foremost, you need to have a mindset of pride, hope, determination, passion, and perseverance, but you also need to have a specific direction, such as setting goals, acquiring foundational skills, and creating a plan of action. Then you need to have the execution to put it into action.

I recommend using one of my favorite formulas: $P = C \times E$. "P" stands for Performance and Results, C stands for Capability or Ability, and E stands for Execution or Action.

In the story of "The Rabbit and the Tortoise," if you are like the Rabbit, no matter how extraordinary your abilities may be, you getting lazy and failing to execute will result in failure. On the other hand, if you are like the tortoise, even with less capability, consistent effort and execution can lead to meaningful results, albeit on a smaller scale.

If we change the "P" in the formula above to "Professional," the conclusion is that by adding the best execution to your abilities and skills, you become a true professional, an expert. I hope we can all strive to live by this formula-simple, but not easy.

Harmonization of the Viewpoint

I don't understand what my dad is telling me

My two daughters, now grown and established in their professional fields, were in middle and high school at the time, and I wanted to support them in their education. I had studied chemical and industrial engineering in college, and in my early professional life I was an engineer, so I was relatively confident in math among other subjects. So, I decided to teach my daughters math and developed a plan to do so.

However, I soon encountered two problems. First, math terminologies in English were unfamiliar to me, and the American way of conceptualizing and solving problems was different from the Korean way as well. My daughters were confused by the difference between the way they were taught in school and my teaching method. My pure intentions and sincerity turned into a subtle conflict between father and daughters. I realized that a different approach might be necessary, so I spoke openly and gently with my daughters, looking for a new path forward.

"Do you think what Dad taught you is, helpful?"

Although I somewhat expected it, I got negative feedback from my daughters.

"The way solving the math is different, and I don't understand what Dad tells me."

"I agree, and you keep telling me I can't do it, which makes it scary and not fun. I don't want to learn this way. I'd rather go to a private academy like "Princeton Review" like my friends."

I was quietly saddened that they did not understand my feelings, but I began exploring new ways to make math more enjoyable for them. I specifically investigated the company called "Princeton Review."

First, I checked out the training program on the website and then visited a nearby academy to make inquiries. I noticed that they were frequently hiring tutors, and after careful consideration, I decided to apply for a tutor position to gain insight into their teaching methods and programs. After that, I went to a nearby school at a designated time for a hiring test. There were about 500 applicants there, and we took a math exam that lasted about two hours. A week later, I received an email with my initial acceptance notice and an announcement about an orientation. I followed the announcement to a location

Eye level synchonization.

I visited with about 100 other initial successful candidates. In the morning, we received training on teaching methods and content, and in the afternoon, we were asked to demonstrate our teaching skills as if we were Princeton Review teachers, based on what we had learned in the morning. The lecture demonstration was part of the hiring process, and Princeton Review managers evaluated and eliminated those who were not qualified. Fortunately, I passed and after about a month of additional tutor training, I was finally able to secure a position as one of 40 part-time tutors.

I showed my daughters my Princeton Review Instructor Certificate and suggested they study math again with me based on the Princeton Review's textbook-centered pedagogy and content standards. They accepted, and the educational support for my daughters concluded just as positively as I had hoped. My family's praise and appreciation for my efforts made the experience even more fulfilling, leaving me with a deep sense of accomplishment.

Two key lessons emerged from this case. First, I succeeded in helping my daughters better understanding the American education system by viewing it from their perspective rather than through my own insistence or stubbornness. Second, my sincere effort as both a father and a tutor strengthened the love and trust between us.

The same applies to our social life. The "Eye Level Synchronization" benefits effective communication and good relationships between friends, acquaintances, colleagues, superiors and subordinates.

Eye-level synchronization consists of four essential elements. The level of competence (knowledge and skills), experience (or background), personality, and motivation which must be considered collectively. Here is how to align these elements.

First, assess the level and content of the four elements for both yourself and your counterpart, a process I call "mutual adjustment readiness levels." This involves evaluating readiness and gaps in knowledge, experience, personality, and interest in the communication topic for both parties.

Second, understand that if you are leading the communication or interaction, the standard of readiness should be based on the other person, not yourself.

Third, initiate your communication and interaction at the other person's eye level and maintain the flow of the conversation.

Fourth, once rapport is established, carefully align your level of readiness with the other person's, making adjustments to synchronize effectively at key moments.

Individuals exhibit varying levels of expertise and proficiency across diverse domains of knowledge and skill sets. The experience gained through social and organizational life differ significantly, as do factors such as age and status. Personalities also vary, spanning a spectrum from extroverted to introverted and positive to negative. Moreover, factors like motivation, interest, needs, proactivity, and enthusiasm reflect varying degrees of spontaneity and engagement among individuals.

However, when addressing problems or challenges at home, work, or within organizations, parents, executives, managers, and others often tackle these issues based on their individual levels of readiness.

This is evident in the interaction between a rambunctious

> "
> The four essential elements to eye-level synchronization
> are the levels of competence, experience, personality, and motivation
> which must be considered collectively.
> "

three-year-old and their mother. Most parents don't try to calm or discipline their young children with logic and rational reasons, nor do they expect immediate acknowledgement of fault, remorse, or improved behavior. Instead, the mother understands her child's level of readiness and chooses the simplest and quickest way to persuade them.

Of course, in this example, if the difference in levels is clear and the leading person has a much higher level of readiness, achieving harmonious eye-level synchronization is relatively easy. However, company dynamics are often complex, making it challenging to assess mutual readiness and achieving eye-level synchronization. When a supervisor or manager assigns a task based on their own expectations and level of readiness without considering the other person's, it often leads to dissatisfaction in communication and strained relationships. Similarly, when a highly competent team member disrespects peers at a similar level, it can create tension and disrupt team dynamics.

Effective communication and strong relationships are built on humility, respect for the others, a win-win mindset, patience, and genuine motivation. The lessons I learned about positive communication and father-daughter relationships that I've learned through my time as a Princeton Review instructor offer concepts and methods that can be applied universally in homes, workplaces organizations, and beyond.

I firmly believe that by practicing eye-level synchronization with introspection, humility, and genuine care for others, we can excel in our roles and foster meaningful connections.

Remember, the world changes depending on your perspective. Standing tall and looking down may offer a limited view, but kneeling and looking up reveals the vast, awe-inspiring sky above.

Change for Improvement and Growth Is Not an Option but Mandatory

Am I the fish in the little pond?

When you work for a company for a certain period, you become familiar not only with your job, but also with the culture of the company, as well as the thoughts, personalities, and work styles of your coworkers. In my case, due to the nature of my work in organizational dynamics and people management, I maintained a constantly updated list of employees in my head, their profiles, personalities, characteristics, strengths, weaknesses, and various aspects of potential. In a similar way, others are continually assessing me as well, each from their own perspective.

Most people are often unaware that they are being evaluated by those who are directly connected to them. However, these informal, covert assessments can offer more objective insights and contribute to personal growth.

As is widely known, there is a practice called "360-degree

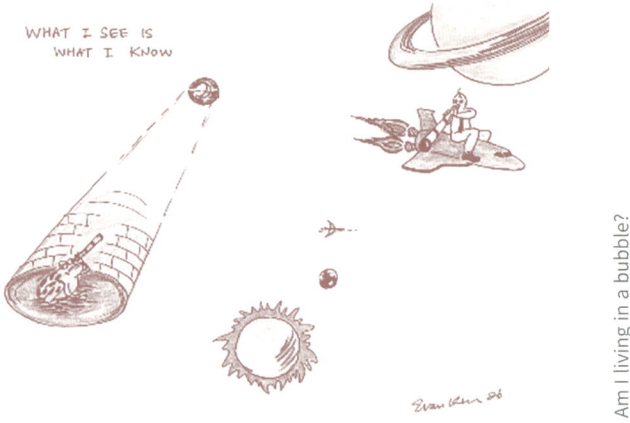

feedback." It is a 360-degree view of yourself, where you are evaluated by people up, down, and across the organization. Many companies are now using 360-degree feedback in parallel with traditional appraisals.

In a typical performance review, quantitative items are listed first for fairness and objectivity. These are usually centered around Key Performance Indicators (KPIs), which are goals set at the beginning of the year in the form of an index. To these are added qualitative factors that are not easily measurable, such as work ethics and attitude, communication, relationships.

In typical 360-degree feedback within the organization, qualitative criteria tend to be more heavily weighted. The reviewee's attitude, demeanor, communication, relationships, leadership, and alignment with company values and culture within the organization could be quite subjective, depending on who conducts the review. However, when opinions are gathered from various functions and many reviewers, the results become relatively meaningful and objective, even though the criteria may be subjective.

360-degree feedback is anonymous, and the results are communicated to the reviewee. It provides valuable insight into how others perceive you and allows employees to be honestly and clearly identify their strengths, weaknesses, and areas for improvement while comparing them to their self-assessments.

The expected outcome of 360-degree feedback is self-reflection and improvement through the evaluation of employees. However, some reviewers' qualities and emotional involvement can also have the side effect of victimizing the reviewee in a witch-hunt style, so care must be taken when conducting the process and collecting results.

In 360-degree feedback, we tend to be harsh and critical of others, but relatively generous and friendly when it comes to evaluating ourselves. Because our self-evaluations are mostly positive, it is not uncommon for them to be quite different from how others have rated us.

A particularly problematic type of self-assessment is the

"manager who does not know what they do not know." Whether it is due to ignorance, overconfidence, or laziness, they do not have a good grasp of their strengths and weaknesses, yet they pretend they know everything. If they are left unadvised or unchallenged, the problem can only escalate. Especially if their position is influential, such as a key executive, the organization is likely to face negative consequences, both tangible and intangible. Employee dissatisfaction and silence may increase, leading to a decline in organizational morale and productivity. Talented employees might leave, leaving behind a workforce that is tailored to suit the boss or remain subservient. These examples are not only common in modern organizations but also throughout history.

There is an old proverb, "The fish in the little pond." In Korean, a similar proverb would be "우물 안 개구리 (oomool an gaeguri: a frog in a well)." In management terms, this can be described as a "paradigm": a person perceives the world inside their pond or well as the whole world. Paradigms are otherwise defined as stereotypes. They are thoughts and behaviors that you take for granted, and they are also ideologies and dispositions that manifest as your existence and identity. Like a fish in the little pond, a person who stays inside their paradigm and thinks the little pond is the only world is bound to have a disconnected

> "
> Change is a process that happens
> when you recognize where you are and then approach
> it with a sense of humility, positivity, and a desire
> to improve and grow.
> "

worldview. Historically, Heungseon Daewongun, who was the prime minister during the late Joseon Dynasty, insisted on a closed-door policy, refusing to engage in trade or diplomatic relations with other countries. This could be an example of the negative aspects of a paradigm. Due to this policy, Korea faced the unfortunate consequence of being colonized by Japan in the early 20th century.

The phrase "it is not the strong one who survives, but the one who changes survives" is a wake-up call to anyone stuck in their rut, like the fish in the little pond. In today's rapid changing world—shaped by evolving societies, economies, technologies, and generations—constant self-examination and improvement are not optional but a necessity.

Of course, in organizations, especially larger ones, implementing changes is difficult even when the need is clear.

That is why change must begin at the top to be implemented swiftly and effectively. Just as adults set examples at home by making judgments and decisions on major issues, in the workplace, leadership's willingness and commitment to change often inspire the organization and its employees to follow suit.

If a company is at the crossroads of change and improvement, it must be communicated to the organization in a positive, rational, logical, common-sense, and human way. At the same time, the initiation of change and improvement must come from the top, including the CEO. If you do not genuinely strive to change and improve yourself but instead merely order your team to do so, they may reluctantly and temporarily comply with your authority. However, such efforts are unlikely to yield lasting or meaningful results.

When individuals or organizations start a new year, they often set new goals. While quantitative goals can be effectively implemented, non-metric objectives such as leadership, relationships, execution, and mindset are subjective and relative, making them challenging to establish and evaluate. As a result, non-metric objectives often don't move beyond the conceptual stage and the results are often superficial. Therefore, it is best to simplify and visualize non-metric goals as actionable to-do lists that are quantifiable, realistic, and grounded in common sense, making them easy to share with the people responsible for driving them.

Change begins by recognizing where you are and approaching it with humility, positivity, and a desire for growth. Once you adopt these attitudes, it is essential to organize your reasons, objectives, and action steps, to set the stage for meaningful improvement.

From there, it is only a matter of time before you effectively experience real, positive change.

The Distance Between Colleagues

Treat like a fireplace

We know that human relationships have a significant impact on society, organizations, and our daily lives. A prominent U.S. research institute has been studying the impact of friendly relationships on companies for years.

Research shows that people feel more connected in a company when they share similar experiences, educational backgrounds, fashion, and values, such as having worked for the same company in the past or belonging to the same hobby club.

The beauty of close relationships is that when things get tough, they support and encourage each other to get through it. They also try to help each other in a positive and proactive manner when cooperating in work. On the other hand, the disadvantage is that they waste work time unnecessarily for personal reasons. They also share complaints, rumors, slander as a way of seeking sympathy and consolation for negative experiences within the organization, such as perceived unfair treatment or conflicts with disliked coworkers. In addition, private groups are formed within the organization, and situations such as competition, jealousy, and slander between groups occur.

I have encountered the phenomenon described in the study during my professional career, and it brings to mind an anecdote from my time at an American company.

A woman called "J" worked in a company's sales support department for many years. One day, another woman, "R," joined the department. During a conversation, J and R realized they were college classmates and hit it off. J and R became like siblings, sharing meals and leaving work together.

J and R found a shared sense of affiliation and security through their identification as college alumni and members of the same department. This phenomenon is also observed among recruits in unions, special forces like the military, and even in gangs.

However, the relationship between J and R began to sour when they were promoted at the same time after their year-end performance review. From J's perspective, R's promotion was unfair. No matter how much experience R had at other companies, J was the senior person at her current company, so the fact that she was promoted at the same time as R made her feel relatively undervalued. J began to resent the favors she had been doing for R and even suspected that R of flattering her manager.

Frustrated, J expressed her feelings toward R in a negative way. J started gossiping about R behind her back, and eventually, R was bullied in a private group that J belonged to. After that, J and R didn't engage in any dialogue with each other, and even their work communications were limited to email, causing their coworkers to feel like they were walking on eggshells around them.

Later, the tension in their uncomfortable relationship led to an incident that violated company policy, resulting in their simultaneous termination.

Treat your colleagues like a fireplace.

J and R's relationship, which they had perceived as a friendship, deteriorated after their promotions. Envy, backstabbing, and conflict ultimately took a toll on both them and the organization. Perhaps their relationship lacked depth, serving merely as an outlet for loneliness and other negative emotions within the workplace.

No matter how close you are, conflicts still can arise, so it's important to remain mindful. Even couples who have been together for a lifetime may argue over the smallest remarks. The saying, "Treat your friends like a stove," captures this balance: if you get too close, you risk being burned by the heat, but if you stay too far away, you lose the warmth altogether.

When coworkers maintain friendly relationships, communication flows easily, and collaboration thrives. However, if the relationship becomes too close, it can blur professional boundaries, potentially leading to the covering up of mistakes and shortcomings. Such dynamics can also create tension within the organization. Inappropriate relationships may arise, especially when informal titles like "big brother" or "big sister" are used, further complicating professional interactions.

A company's primary goal is to generate profit alongside achieving other objectives. Therefore, it's not ideal for employees to prioritize personal relationships over fulfilling their roles

> "
> Social life is a series of connections:
> Some of which begin as coincidences,
> some of which develop into bonds, some of which are isolated,
> and only a few of which become inevitable.
> "

and responsibilities. It's more logical for employees to focus on maximizing their responsibilities and exercising their authority while at the company, and to leave at a time that is appropriate for both the employee and the organization.

Although coworker relationships may seem enduring, it's common for people to part ways for various reasons. When a coworker leaves, a farewell dinner is often held, and promises to stay in touch are made. However, these connections tend to fade quickly. Once the shared goal of work disappears, the bond weakens, naturally return to their separate paths.

Humans are social animals, thriving on interaction and cooperation. Social life is built on a series of connections. Some begin as coincidences and may develop into stronger bonds, while many eventually fade for various reasons. Only a select few evolve into lasting friendships or unbreakable ties.

Developing wise relationship skills is crucial for success. Within an organization, maintaining strong professional and personal connections is essential for the growth and well-being of both the company and its employees. While making a positive first impression is important, departing on good terms is even more crucial. Neglecting relationships simply because there's nothing more to give is unwise.

No one knows what lies ahead. There is a saying that goes, "There are no permanent friends and no permanent enemies." It is a bittersweet sentiment, suggesting a business world devoid of loyalty, where alliances and friendships are formed out of necessity.

You spend more than half of your day at work. When you have coworkers who respect, understand, and support you with advice and encouragement, your life becomes enriched beyond the scope of work. Such colleagues enhances your overall well-being. This remind me of a quote from French writer Albert Camus.

> Do not walk behind me. I may not be able to lead.
> Do not walk in front of me. I may not be able to follow.
> Just walk beside me and be my friend.

An Attitude of a Leader with Dignity

"Stand" makes Leader 101 a reality

I remember a company year-end party many years ago, and an employee who was hosting circulated questionnaires ahead of time for a game we were going to play at the party. The questionnaires asked a few questions and one of the questions was "Which part of your body are you most grateful for?" I thought long and hard about it and wrote "the soles of my feet." Later at the party, the host pointed at me and asked why I answered, "The soles of my feet," I explained the reasoning behind my answer.

"There are many organs in our bodies that are often given special mention, like our eyes, nose, and mouth. But the soles of our feet are at the bottom of the body, so it is hard to see them when we are standing, so we often forget about them. And yet, without us realizing it, the soles of our feet are the starting point of support that keeps our whole body upright and active."

Of course, I highlighted the importance of the soles of the feet, but I also wanted to symbolically emphasize the value of those who quietly do their jobs in the shadows. Additionally, I wanted to explore the concept of "how we walk through life," a topic I frequently discuss in my leadership and interpersonal training sessions.

Humans live their lives in a standing, sitting, or lying position. During periods of active social engagement, we often spend a lot of time on our feet, standing and moving around. The way someone stands and moves can offer subtle insights into their mindset, reflecting their confidence, openness, or discomfort in the situation.

For example, when soldiers or cadets stand proudly during a ceremonial drill with their chests puffed out, their backs

Stand firm!

erect, and their eyes fierce, we see confidence, strength, and determination. On the other hand, if a person is barely standing with hunched shoulders and a hunched back, we can detect vulnerability, depression, and anxiety.

The way we stand, walk, and run symbolizes productive activity. Imagine ourselves standing, walking, and running across different parts of the world, engaging in diverse social activities. Since all training sessions are conducted in English, I would like to focus on the word "stand" and weave the message around it by pairing it with other impactful words. My goal is to use these compound words to convey a meaningful message, starting with the question, "How do you stand in life?"

"Stand in the foreground" and "Stand in the background"

As the main actors on the stage of life, they seek to impress the audience by standing in the foreground with spotlight, and when their time is up, they hope to leave to applause. However, most of us overlook the actors who are standing in the background, who invest just as much time and sacrifice, yet quietly exit the stage when the curtain falls, receiving little attention or appreciation.

Therefore, we should aim to be leaders who make the most of our time, but we must remember that leadership demands hard work and sacrifice, often involving significant challenges and pains.

"Stand under" and "Stand above"

Are you standing under someone or above someone?

When we lower ourselves, we naturally elevate those around us. Standing under signifies humbly placing your ego and self-respect below those of others. This requires considerable patience and discipline. However, in the end, much like the seesaw principle, both you and the others can rise higher together. Through this process, you will earn the goodwill, trust, and respect of those around you.

In contrast, when we elevate ourselves, we naturally lower those around us. If you are knowledgeable, capable, or hold a managerial or leadership position, it can be easy to become arrogant and domineering, sometimes even taking such behavior for granted. However, when you wield power and status to lord over others, it becomes nearly impossible to inspire genuine loyalty of followership.

"Understand"

Reversing the word order of "stand under" transforms it into "understand," emphasizing the deep connection between

> "The word "stand" is deeply associated with an attitude toward life, as well as growing as a leader of character."

humility and comprehension.

We often use the phrase "I understand" mechanically in conversations and meetings, without really giving it much thought. However, it is not uncommon for situations to arise where we do not exactly understand each other's expectations.

This is because people put their ego and self-respect above caring and respect for the other person, so they do not listen to what is being said and only remember what they want to hear. Or they have already made up their minds and simply go through the motions of formal conversation, without genuine engagement.

If we lower ourselves to a "stand under" attitude, we can give our attention and care to what the other person is saying and truly understand their meaning and intent.

"Standard"

When "ard" is added to the word "stand," it signifies a criterion, measure, or benchmark often associated with expectations or norms. We need clear standards and principles when reflecting on the question, "how do I stand in life?" In social and organizational life, we often see people who are strict with others but lax with themselves. When things go wrong, they blame the other person or the situation, not themselves. They also tend to be reluctant to accept criticism of their faults or shortcomings.

However, successful or respected leaders are often their own toughest critics. Achieving top leadership positions in the world demands relentless hard work, continuous self-improvement, and maintaining high standards for both motivation and self-care.

"Standout"

The challenging standards you set for yourself, your positive attitude, and the results of persistent efforts are realized as a competitive advantage. Competitive advantage is the ability to "stand out" in the public eye and be recognized for excellence. Society or an organization puts people with these qualifications and skills at the forefront, calling them leaders and naturally giving them the roles they deserve.

The key concepts related to "stand" that we discussed earlier, when applied effectively, will ultimately earn you the respect to "outstand." To summarize: Take pride in standing at the foreground, humble yourself (stand under), strive to empathize with and understand others (understand), elevate your management principles and benchmarks (standard), and excel as a leader in both social and organizational settings (stand out). Those who consistently embody these principles are truly "Outstanding!" and worthy of admiration.

The word "stand" is closely tie to the question, "How will you stand in life?" and reflects the stance needed to grow as a leader of character. As we navigate through life, it is crucial to remind ourselves daily of the significance of "stand"—to take a stand, move forward, and strive to achieve the goals we have set for ourselves.

The Lubricant of Relationships

Who will welcome me?

In our social lives, there are some people we look forward to seeing and others we are reluctant to meet. Amid our busy lives, certain people linger in our memories positively, even if we haven't shared much interaction or communication with Their presence can evoke a sense of comfort and nostalgia, sometimes inspiring us to reach out and reconnect.

On the other hand, negative memories that trouble you and weigh you down are the ones you prefer to avoid, even when they surface in your mind.

We believe that a relationship is an essential interaction between two or more people working together to fulfill their life purposes and goals. They connect through shared values, culture, work, finances, politics, religion, and other factors to meet each other's needs within their community and society. This underscores why building positive and meaningful relationships is such an important, life-enhancing endeavor.

Our social lives take various forms shaped by the choices and decisions we make. Much of this is influenced by the roles we play within specific locations and groups. However, some individuals find themselves thrust into unwanted situations by societal or organizational pressures, often beyond their control or capacity.

Relationships can be formed based on visible factors like education, wealth, and power, as well as invisible elements such as values, personality, and preferences. While relationships can have deeper conceptual and philosophical purposes, they often exist for practical reasons—social survival, mutual benefit, alliances, and the pursuit of resources through competitive advantage.

Relationships are not always positive; they can also bring challenges and conflicts. We often hear about incidents of blackmail, assault, disclosure, and litigation in relationships. These stem from impure motives and intentions in forming the relationship, and from the pursuit of goals that are deviant, unethical, or illegal. Furthermore, when tangible and intangible resources are not fairly distributed to meet the goals of both parties, the relationship may end, and sometimes with attempts to harm the other party.

Some relationships are more approachable than others, which

What are the remedies for relationships?

I refer to as interpersonal relationships. These relationships focus less on quantifying and judging, and more on sharing emotions, thoughts, feelings, and common values such as love, friendship, happiness, and faith, rather than pursuing worldly goals.

Interpersonal relationships do not need to be formal or centered around posturing and prestige. They shouldn't require mind-reading or constant vigilance. Instead, they should focus on mutual reliance, fostering a sense of unity and belonging—this is what we truly aspire to in human connections.

Of course, misunderstandings and conflicts can arise from a lack of sensitivity and shared emotions, sometimes turning a friendly relationship irrevocably sour.

Relationships are a vital part of social life and should not be taken lightly. Those who excel in managing them are more likely to earn respect and recognition within an organization. So, what are essential "relationship lubricants" needed to foster positive connections?

First, respect is essential. You should relate to others as equals, regardless of their position in society and the organization. This involves avoiding arrogance and superiority, and instead, practicing moderation (中庸). Moderation is an attitude that embraces, avoiding extremes or bias. By being moderate, you can connect with a wide range of people, especially when you show humility and respect for those in positions of authority.

Second, practice faithfulness (信義). Faithfulness combines faith and loyalty, meaning you should trust others and act in a way that earns their trust in return. A deep relationship cannot thrive without mutual trust and the ability to keep promises. Honesty serves as the foundation for genuine loyalty and faithfulness.

Third, be sincere and caring. Avoid being overly formal and speak genuinely from the heart. While it may not be possible to love everyone, cultivating tolerance is essential. Tolerance involves generous acceptance and a willingness to forgive. When you genuinely care about others, understanding naturally develops, and this understanding can deepens into compassion.

> "
> There is no definitive roadmap to building strong human relationships. Instead, they require a genuine willingness to find common ground and work towards mutual understanding.
> "

Fourth, good manners and effective communication are essential. Demonstrating basic etiquette, situational awareness, and sound judgment are key to fostering meaningful connections. Be genuine, prioritize uplifting others, and extend thoughtful compliments while using respectful language. Whenever possible, steer clear of accusations and criticisms; instead, build rapport by breaking the ice with smiles and laughter. Maintaining "eye contact" is also vital for establishing and sustaining effective communication.

There is no definitive roadmap to building strong human relationships. They aren't achieved through theoretical knowledge, information, strategy, or technology. Instead, they require a genuine willingness to find common ground and work towards mutual understanding. This effort must be continuous, internalizing attitudes that serve as the "lubricant of relationships."

At times, I find myself flipping through the business cards I've collected over my career, reflecting on the people behind them—wondering who would welcome me warmly and who might not. It serves as a humbling reminder that while projecting a positive image in our relationships is important, it's the sincerity, honesty, and genuine care we show behind the scenes that truly build lasting connections.

The Give-and-Take Formula

Are you giving to receive or receiving to give?

Our lives are a series of give-and-take interactions, which I also refer to as "sharing." In this context, sharing involves the exchange of certain elements with individuals who are open to sharing a part of themselves, whether on a physical or emotional level.

In our daily lives, we alternate between being givers or takers, depending on the situation. Historically, bartering has been the primary means of trade among humans. Similarly, countries and organizations engage in give-and-take with their citizens and employees. States provide entitlements and rights to citizens, offering protection within the system in exchange for taxes. Organizations offer salaries, benefits, promotions, and recognition to employees, who in return contribute performance, experience, and effort.

However, the give-and-take principle can be misused in unethical situations. For example, robbers use threats and scammers use lies to extort money. Naturally, they face legal consequences for their actions.

There are exceptions to the principle of give-and-take, particularly in relationships like those between a husband and wife, or a parent and child. Parents provide physical and emotional support to their children out of love, and in return, they may experience joy or anxiety. These exchanges are driven by love and occur without expectations or formal agreements, making imbalances in give-and-take less problematic. Religion is another area where the give-and-take formula doesn't easily apply.

A long time ago, I was on a business trip to South Korea and stopped by a department store. The line at the gift card section was long, with many people buying 100,000 won gift cards in bundles (100,000 won is about 75 in US Dollars.). This was before the Kim Young-ran Act, a law prohibiting government employees from accepting improper solicitations or gifts. I wondered who would receive bundles of 100,000-won gift certificates. As it seemed beyond common sense to give such a gift without expecting something in return.

To varying degrees, much of social life on a give-and-take basis. Throughout human history, the equation has always been about balancing the quantity and quality on both sides, seeking mutual and equal satisfaction. In the modern world, however, this equation is often calculated, bring with it the temptation to give less and take more.

In the past, some Confucian Koreans criticized American give-and-take as materialistic and selfish. American society tends to quantify and balance give-and-take transactions, aiming for fairness.

Americans aim seek to maximize their value and rights in these exchanges, and if they feel wronged, they're quick to pursue legal action. This approach tends to foster clear and transparent interactions.

The phrase "give and take" highlights the importance of giving before receiving, and genuine sharing occurs when both aspects harmoniously come together.

The best form of sharing is unconditional, heartfelt, and pure-giving without expecting anything in return. While sharing can involve material aspects, the most meaningful exchanges are

Formula for give and take.

emotional, encompassing love, care, and concern. The ideal form of sharing balances minimal material exchange with maximum heartfelt connection.

Every holiday season, we send and receive Christmas and greeting cards. However, in recent years, handwritten letters and cards have become less common as smartphone—centric social networks have taken over. In today's age of convenience, many people send Christmas and greeting cards with just a simple message or signature on the pre-printed content. What do you think or feel when you receive such mailings? Personally, I didn't feel much; it often seems like generic gesture, as if I'm just one of many recipients the sender is greeting out of habit.

For many of us, the end of the year and the beginning of a new one hold a special significance. Personally, I find it difficult to let this time pass without doing something meaningful, which is why I decided to organize my activities with the aim of spreading warmth and kindness.

Every November, I reflect on the year, compile a list of people I've connected with, thoughtfully note the messages I want to convey, and carefully select the appropriate cards and gifts for each recipient. Once I have done this before Thanksgiving, I set aside a half-day on a Friday during the holiday season to write handwritten letters, referencing the messages I have already prepared. I experienced the satisfying ache of my fingers as I wrote more than 100 handwritten letters. Each card and gift was then mailed or hand-delivered to ensure it reached the recipient during the first week of December.

What started as a pure act of kindness has now become an annual tradition for me, and while the time and expense involved in preparing everything is not insignificant, it is nothing compared to the joy and reward that comes with it.

We deeply value the tangible and intangible outcomes of our hard work, and frugality is one of those important life lessons. We often notice people around us who are careful with their spending, whether it's being mindful of their purchases at the market or using coupons they've diligently saved. They make the most of what they have.

But what's truly remarkable is that some of the most frugal people, when they see someone in need, give without hesitation. It's the small, selfless gestures from those who have less that truly warm our hearts. These acts of kindness are far more beautiful than large donations made for tax benefits or to show-off, leaving a lasting imprint on our souls.

I believe human relationships are shaped more by the "immaterial heart" that lies beneath the "material give and take." This kind of sharing is immeasurable, beyond calculation, and

> "
> In English, it is written as "give and take" and not "take and give," because give comes first and take comes second.
> "

lacks a universal standard. It's guided by each person's unique values, thoughts, and feelings, which are communicated in ways that touch the heart, transcending any material exchange.

Typically, we spend about 45 years engaged in productive activity and income generation, starting in our early 20s and continuing into our mid-60s. Throughout this time, we interact with countless individuals within for-profit and non-profit organizations, shaping the fabric of our business, social, and professional lives. Among the most frequent and impactful activities during this period is the exchange of goods, services, and values with those we encounter. Reflecting on these years, it becomes clear that our lives are deeply etched with the marks of countless acts of give-and-take.

Each interaction, each exchange, weaves a thread in the tapestry of our existence, leaving behind traces that define our careers and shape the essence of who we are. Looking back, I realize these exchanges are not merely transactions; they are meaningful connections that have left an indelible impact on the journey of my life

We live in a materialistic world where sharing benefits is essential for survival and success, particularly in political, economic, and organizational contexts. While material exchanges are inevitable, it's the quality and depth of non-material give-and-take that truly elevate and enrich relationships.

The ideal relationship is pure, warm, and focused on giving rather than receiving. This approach fosters connections that resemble family bonds and close friendships.

Conversely, self-centeredness and a lack of gratitude often lead to family discord, isolation from friends, and conflicts at work-symptoms of a mindset focused on taking rather than giving.

Those who embrace values like service, dedication, and sacrifice often find that the joy of giving surpasses the joy of receiving. Phrases like "What you give out, you get back," and "What seems like a loss at the time, is a gain in the end." Reflecting this belief, I aspire to shift from a mindset of "giving to get" to one of "giving willingly," embracing the genuine joy of life. My goal is to become someone who gives freely and empties myself for the benefit of others, rather than focusing on taking and filling. I aim to offer time and care generously, even if it means being perceived as a bit naive.

Basics

Never let your guard down

We often hear the phrase "get back to basics" in our social and professional lives, and when we make plans or resolutions for the new year, we often talk about getting back to basics.

Basics (初心) means "first thoughts" in Chinese characters. However, my interpretation of "Basics" refers to maintaining the original perspective and passion you had when starting something new, along with the initial motivation or purpose. If you are following through on what you set out to do, there is no need to make an extra effort to appear determined. However, when things don't go as planned, we often start searching for solutions and may need to revisit our original intent.

The initial mindset, though it varies from person to person, is often characterized by a sense of urgency, determined attitude, and a strong resolve to plan, execute, and achieve results in challenging situations that demand confidence and commitment. For example, the enthusiasm of young people taking their first steps in life, the determination of founders starting a business, and the dedication of entrepreneurs striving to build a global company—all of these are examples of the initial mindset (初心). This mindset embodies the passion, resolve, and drive that are present at the beginning of any significant journey. Once goals are achieved, many feel a sense of satisfaction and gratitude, enjoying the praise and admiration of others. However, some begin to relax and grow complacent. The initial urgency that fueled their efforts often diminishes amidst their tangible and intangible successes, giving way to complacency, laziness, and even arrogance.

Maybe that's where the phrase "never let your guard down" comes from. In boxing, the guard is the basic stance where you

Yearning and Desperation.

keep your arms up to block your opponent's punches. Without this basic stance, you will never win because you will not be able to protect your face and your stomach.

When you're cold, you truly appreciate the warmth of home, and when you are hungry, every meal is a delight. From that perspective, the hardships of the past nourish the gratitude of the present.

However, we must be cautious of complacency. It's like sitting on the couch and watching TV until you gradually slide down and end up lying flat. Once you indulge in the comfort of complacency, you're tempted to seek even more ease, and before long, laziness becomes a part of your daily routine.

We are naturally drawn to familiar routines and habits out of inertia. However, this comfort in certainty and predictability makes it difficult to foster change, improvement, or innovation.

When I interview candidates for entry-level positions fresh out of college, I often find them to be highly motivated and enthusiastic, asking challenging and positive questions.

However, I've noticed that some of these new hires, after two or three years, lose their motivation, enthusiasm, and the innocence and honesty they once had. They begin to blame the outside world or others for their poor performance or results. I believe that the loss of innocence plays a significant role in this

> If you want to stay focused in life, you have to develop the right habits. It is not to act on a thought that pops into your head once or twice; it is much more important and difficult to do it consistently.

shift.

At the beginning of each new year, many companies have kickoff ceremonies where executives announce their plans, resolutions, and mantras, though these can sometimes amount to little more than lip service. I recall an executive who, year after year, promised to return to the initial mindset but never followed through, leaving me to question his sincerity. His mental complacency remained unchanged. While resolutions were mentioned, they often seemed more like self-serving declarations meant to boost his ego and save face in front of his team. If you make resolutions without genuine intent and effort, you're likely to end the year with nothing but excuses and regrets.

I fully agree with the saying, "Doing nothing is also a habit." To stay focused in life, you must cultivate the right habits. It's not about acting on a thought that comes to mind once or twice—it's about the consistency that truly matters, and it's far more challenging.

Research shows that it takes 66 days to form a lasting habit. If you can stick to a plan for that long, your body and mind will adapt, making even the hardest tasks feel achievable. Success becomes a habit, not just a goal.

It is never too late. If you find yourself off course, don't give up—go back to your roots, where you were authentic, and start again. That's how you live a life without regrets.

The Class of Leaders Who Will Set Nations and Organizations Right

Wisdom, Trust, Humanity, Discipline, Courage

Since my college years, I have followed Korean and American politics, economics, and society, eventually broadening my interest to include global affairs.

Countries and organizations have leaders who represent and serve their people and constituents, such as politicians, senior government officials, social impact activists and CEOs. They lead with a sense of duty and responsibility, striving to guide their countries, societies and organizations in the right direction. As representatives of the rights and responsibilities of their people and constituents, they are held to high moral and ethical standards.

Most leaders understand this responsibility, but unfortunately, some fall into the trap of wielding power over their people and constituents. Through my observations of politicians and high-ranking government officials, I have noticed certain recurring

Wisdom, Trust, Humanity, Discipline, Courage.

behaviors. Here is my personal perspective on them.

First, many of them come from challenging backgrounds. However, their clear sense of purpose and life goals drove them to study diligently, attend prestigious schools, and often take on leadership roles in organizations like student government.

They entered politics with the aim of promoting stability and welfare for the people, envisioning themselves as the right kind of leader. Some were motivated by progress, social movements, or anti-establishment ideals. Along the way, they recognized the need for strong connections and patrons as well as the importance of voters.

They cultivated loyalty by forming close ties with influential mid-level politicians and public officials. While some may have loosened the bonds of nepotism link, it's difficult to verify.

These leaders are willing to make any sacrifice to be elected or promoted. Politicians, in particular, present themselves as candidates of integrity, justice, competence, and experience. They hit the campaign trail, often with their spouses by their side, and make extensive use of the media extensively to promote their image.

However, once elected or promoted, the problems often arise. They no longer maintain a low profile, much like someone struggling with the strain of a herniated disc in their neck.

They dine and travel without paying, often under the guise of official business, and use their position for personal benefits. Some even turn local government offices into errand centers for personal tasks, and their misconduct eventually makes headlines.

They align themselves with factions, adamantly asserting their group's correctness regardless of logic, objectivity, or morality. Policies, ideologies, and tactics stretch and shift like rubber bands, adapting to circumstances. They excel at "otherize" certain groups, rallying people around a "one-team" mentality, only to abandon that unity when it no longer serves their interests.

At a certain point, the behaviors I observed led me to stop

following legislative and administrative coverage in Korean newspapers and news outlets. Unfortunately, when I hear the words "politicians" or "high-ranking officials," what comes to mind are images of incitement, collusion, conspiracy, pettiness, and domination. As a result, I've developed the habit of avoiding discussions about politics in gatherings with colleagues or acquaintances. This indifference seems to come from a sense of disappointment and resignation—that no matter how much we debate and point out what's right and wrong, it changes nothing.

In reality, the political arena is filled with masters of manipulation, engaging in petty factional squabbles at the expense of the nation and it's people. The public, weary of these negative and unethical dramas, has largely disengaged.

It is essential for leaders of nations and organizations to exhibit strong character, uphold their responsibilities, and act with unwavering integrity. This reminds me of the story of SONY, the renowned Japanese electronics company known for revolutionizing personal audio with the iconic Walkman. Often cited in the media, Sony's turnaround from the brink of collapse is a powerful example. Kazuo Hirai, who started as a low-level employee, became CEO in 2012 and successfully transformed SONY from a struggling manufacturer into a profitable

> According to the "The Art of War," a general must possess five qualities: wisdom, faith, humility, courage, and discipline.

business. It is a story that highlights the importance of leaders both in nations and organizations.

Recent political, economic, and social developments in South Korea have further highlighted the importance of leadership. Leaders are pivotal figures who determine the rise or fall of nations and organizations. People entrust them with their vision and promises, living with the hope and expectation of positive outcomes.

Countries and organizations may differ in scale and audience, but their goals, objectives, and methods of achieving them are fundamentally similar. The critical factor in both lies in the leader's attitude and competence. Therefore, I earnestly hope for the happiness of the people of Korea and the members of each organization. I wish for them to find happiness, and I would like to reflect on leadership within this context.

As a leader, your role is to step in front, share your mission, inspire others to join you, and lead by example. However, before presenting your mission, plans, and assignments, it is crucial to follow a process that is logical, rational, realistic, practical, and commonly understood. The next step involves assessing these elements in a way that doesn't overwhelm your people or constituents.

Leaders must present a clear vision for the future, share the mission and specific goals, and lead by example, embodying values such as passion, honesty, resilience, and unity to inspire others to follow. Moreover, they should evaluate outcomes with transparency, reasonableness, and fairness, ensuring accountability at every stage of the process.

Some may argue that this is an idealized and unrealistic view of leadership, but I believe that by striving for these ideals, we can begin to lead with true integrity.

According to the "The Art of War" by Sun Tzu, an ancient Chinese military strategist and philosopher, a general must possess five essential qualities: wisdom, trust, humanity, discipline, and courage. These qualities signify "wisdom and knowledge," "trust and faith," "humility and love," "discipline and law," and "courage and willingness." In this context, the term "general" represents a leader. When leaders embody these traits, the foundation for an ideal nation, society, and organization will naturally emerges.

A Truly Professional Manager

Result = Capability × Execution

I have had the privilege of taking on various roles and responsibilities throughout my organizational career. Attracting, developing, and retaining professional employees is critical to a company's stability, change, and growth. Through professional employees, we can exert strong competitiveness, build a successful company, and ensure that the employees and their families can enjoy a peaceful and fulfilling life.

A professional manager observes, analyzes, evaluates, and anticipates the environment and circumstances to effectively contribute to the company's goals, objectives, and stable growth by fully performing their functions and roles. Coupled with leadership that supports and motivates employees, efficiently and effectively distributes work, and empowers them to achieve maximum results, this creates an ideal environment.

Experts must possess specialized knowledge, skills, and experience in their field, maintaining both absolute and relative competitive advantage. Senior managers, on the other hand, should harness their creativity and dedication to propel the company's growth while fostering the development of its people.

The process of identifying and developing professional manager candidates with these qualifications and requirements mirrors the concept of training a newly commissioned officer in the military to excel in both combat and strategy.

While the qualifications and evaluation criteria for specialists and managers are widely explored in countless management book, there is one fundamental expectation that I emphasize in every training session: "Result = Capability × Execution." This simple yet profound formula encapsulates the essential attributes a company seeks in a professional manager.

This formula applies not only to practical or quantitative situations but also to conceptual or qualitative ones. The essence of the formula is this: No matter how great your abilities are, if you only talk and fail to take action, the result will always be nothing. On the other hand, even if your abilities are modest, taking action will lead to some form of result.

In other words, words alone, no matter how eloquent or plentiful, mean little without tangible, concrete actions to back them up. The outcome depends not just on what you say, but on what you do. If you possess strong competence—such as knowledge, skills, problem-solving abilities, communication, productivity, judgment, and excellence in execution—positive results will naturally follow.

An executive must internalize the formula of "Result = Capability × Execution." However, some managers deviate from this formula and manage to stay afloat, open due to their status and authority. While they may maintain their position, their continued presence harms both the organization and its people. These managers often exhibit the following typical characteristics.

They fail to perform their duties, masking their lack of results with glossy rhetoric, inflating any small contributions they make, and always finding excuses for what they don't accomplish.

When a collaborative project fails, they dodge responsibility by blaming others. They interact with people in an egocentric, authoritarian, high-pressure, one-sided manner, giving unnecessary advice and interfering in tasks beyond their scope.

While management scholars present various theories about the ideal professional manager, and the concepts in management books often sound impressive, they can become confusing when applied to the realities of a rapidly changing workplace. From a practical perspective, I believe the formula "Result = Capability × Execution" provides a clear and effective framework for professional managers.

The keyword in this formula is "execution." A tortoise-like professional manager, who quietly and steadily completes tasks—even at a slower pace—is more likely to achieve better results than a rabbit-like manager who possesses high competence but fails to execute due to complacency or laziness.

To stay focused, I live by two powerful phrases that I emphasize in my training. They "enjoy the pain" and "go it alone like the horns of a moose."

"Enjoy the pain" can be illustrated by the joy of a mother welcoming new life after labor or the triumph of a marathoner crossing the finish line. If you can not only endure pain but also find joy in overcoming it-no matter how lonely, difficult, or

> "Output = Capability × Execution" is the formula you must internalize to become an exceptional professional manager, and the keyword in this formula is "execution."

challenging the situation—you can achieve anything and reach any destination.

The phrase "Go alone, like the horns of a moose," is an expression from the "Sutta Nipata," an early Buddhist text. In this context, the moose (or rhino) symbolizes the seeker of truth, while its horns serve as a reminder to stand firm and move forward with unwavering resolve.

I take this lesson deeply to heart, striving to move forward independently and steadily, without being swayed by the internal and external influences of good or bad, right or wrong, in my thoughts and emotions. In life, while we may occasionally collaborate work with others, much of the time we must make decisions and act independently. The moose's steadfastness in the face of danger and hardship reminds us of the importance of resilience and perseverance in our individual journeys.

Similarly, in the professional realm, possessing the best abilities alone does not define a professional manager. The true measure of a professional manager lies in delivering results through execution, not merely through ideas or words. For "Result = Capability × Execution" to truly serve as a key performance indicator (KPI), you must cultivate a mindset focused on execution. This means clearing out the negative, draining, and emotional weeds from your mental garden and planting seeds of pure purpose and humble goals.

If you aspire to be an expert in management—or a winner in life—you must sharpen your ability to execute. To help with that, I want to leave you with a motivational phrase I often share during my training sessions for professional managers. It's a simple yet profound motto that can also serve as a powerful guide in life: Fast is good. Farther is better. To the end is best.

The Necessity of Non-Business Communication and Relationships

A healthy mind for a healthy body

Throughout my four decades of work, I've made it a rule not to discuss company matters or colleagues with my family. I realized that sharing my personal analysis, judgments, and conclusions could influence my family's perception, leading them to align with my subjective views.

This, in turn, could create misunderstandings about people if my thoughts were biased or strayed from the facts. To prevent this, I consciously avoid bringing work-related stories—especially negative ones—into my home life. In hindsight, the concerns I refrained from sharing never materialized, affirming the value of maintaining this boundary.

That said, my interest in and involvement with the company and its people have always been significant—some might even say excessive. I have a tendency to care about the non-business aspects of people's lives because I've witnesses how these factors can directly influence their performance. With this perspective in mind, I would like to share three stories that highlight the importance of non-business communication fostering meaningful relationships within the workplace.

Gift and a Handwritten Letter

At the start of every new year, I organize the highlights of the year in a notepad on my PC and smartphone including birthdays, anniversaries, hire dates, and social celebrations like Valentine's Day and Halloween. At the beginning of each month, I review these notes to identify special occasions for my employees. I set aside time to prepare meaningful gifts and write handwritten letters to them. It brings me joy and a sense of reward to take time out of my busy schedule to do something thoughtful for my groups.

Through this process, I've been able to build closer, more human relationships with the members, fostering a sense of empathy and connection, almost like a second family. This, in turn, has helped develop a strong sense of professional synergy.

A Healthy Mind in a Healthy Body

I observed one of my group members closely for a while. He had the right skills, attitude, potential, but lacked competitive drive, so I wanted to help him find motivation and set goals.

He loved indulgent foods and avoided exercise, so I explained that developing a competitive spirit comes from challenging oneself and that perseverance starts with self-respect. I also shared the phrase, "a healthy mind in a healthy body" and convinced him to commit to a three-month weight loss project, offering a reward if he succeeded. Three months later, he surpassed his goal, was congratulated by his coworkers, and received a reward. This project helped him break his laziness, boosted his confidence, and ignited a newfound competitive spirit.

Weight Scale and Advice

We had a team member who, during a shower, couldn't even see his own belly button and felt ashamed of his appearance. With my encouragement, he decided to embark on a weight loss journey. However, he fell into what I refer to as the category of a "vague goal seeker"—someone with unclear plans and intentions, which made it difficult to set a clear path toward success.

A healthy mind for a healthy body.

"Vague goal seekers" often use abstract adjectives/adverbs and future tense verbs when talking about their resolutions or goals. They often rely on phrases like "this time," "definitely," and "someday," coupled with future tense verbs like "I'm going to" or "I want to." By avoiding present-tense commitments, they lack a sense of urgency and leave themselves an easy escape route for excuses if they fail.

To help him stay on track, I decided to motivate him through what I call "positive humiliation," though I was careful to control the level.

My tool of choice? A weight scale. I gave him a weight scale that tracked not just weight but body fat, visceral fat, bio-age, and muscle mass. Armed with this, he developed a more concrete plan and stuck to it.

Even though he did not reach his goal within the original timeframe, the changes were remarkable. He made his goals specific, timed, and measurable. With improved execution, he began to see tangible results—not just in his health but in his work as well.

The combination of the gift of a scale and some honest advice set him on a virtuous cycle of planning and execution. Over time, he transformed from a vague goal-seeker into a proactive individual who sets and accomplishes clear, action-oriented goals.

As demonstrated in these examples, both my team members and I experienced improved performance on subsequent tasks after completing individual projects. Supporting and engaging employees in the non-business aspects of their lives—though it can sometimes feel mentally and physically taxing or even be perceived as intrusive—is essential. When managers and employees foster connections beyond work-related tasks, they significantly enhance their effectiveness. This is why I continually stress the importance of non-business communication and relationships in cultivating a thriving and productive organizational culture.

First, through non-work communication, you can better understand each other's personal and professional values, perspectives, expectations. As you get to know one another, preconceived notions, grievances, and misunderstandings gradually fade away, fostering a more positive and aligned relationship without the need for explicit discussion.

Next, non-business communication fosters a sense of connection and belonging. Your coworkers are like a second family. You spend a significant part of your day together, working towards organizational goals and fostering a shared culture. These non-business interactions naturally enhance collaboration, creating a more supportive and empowering environment.

Additionally, it fosters mutual education. Team members can share positive experiences, knowledge, and insights, contributing

> "
> The reason managers support and engage their employees in non-business aspects of their lives is that their employees are more effective when they have that connection and relationship.
> "

to both personal and professional growth. In this environment, you can exchange gifts, letters, and learn valuable personal qualities like sincerity, empathy, consideration, sharing, and gratitude.

Lastly, non-business communication serves as a mirror, enabling self-reflection on your actions and presence. Building relationships and maintaining ongoing communication must be rooted in trust and respect. For this to happen, your thoughts and actions need to be positively perceived by others, as coworkers are always observing one another. To be an effective leader, you must align your words and actions, practicing consistent self-management to provide credible and persuasive guidance. In this way, non-business communication acts as a barometer, gauging the appropriateness of one's behavior and words.

Over my 40 years of working life, I've witnessed countless gifts and handwritten letters exchanged during anniversaries, Valentine's Day, Thanksgiving, and Christmas. These small gestures may seem fleeting, but they leave a lasting impact. Through these exchanges, I've also been fortunate to receive numerous gifts and cards. Nowadays, I find myself digitally scanning and organizing these cards appreciating the heartfelt sentiments they hold.

In this way non-business communication and relationships are imbued with sincerity and a personal philosophy toward both people and work. I've come to understand that these gestures are more than just a means of connecting with others—they are also a reflection of my own life and journey.

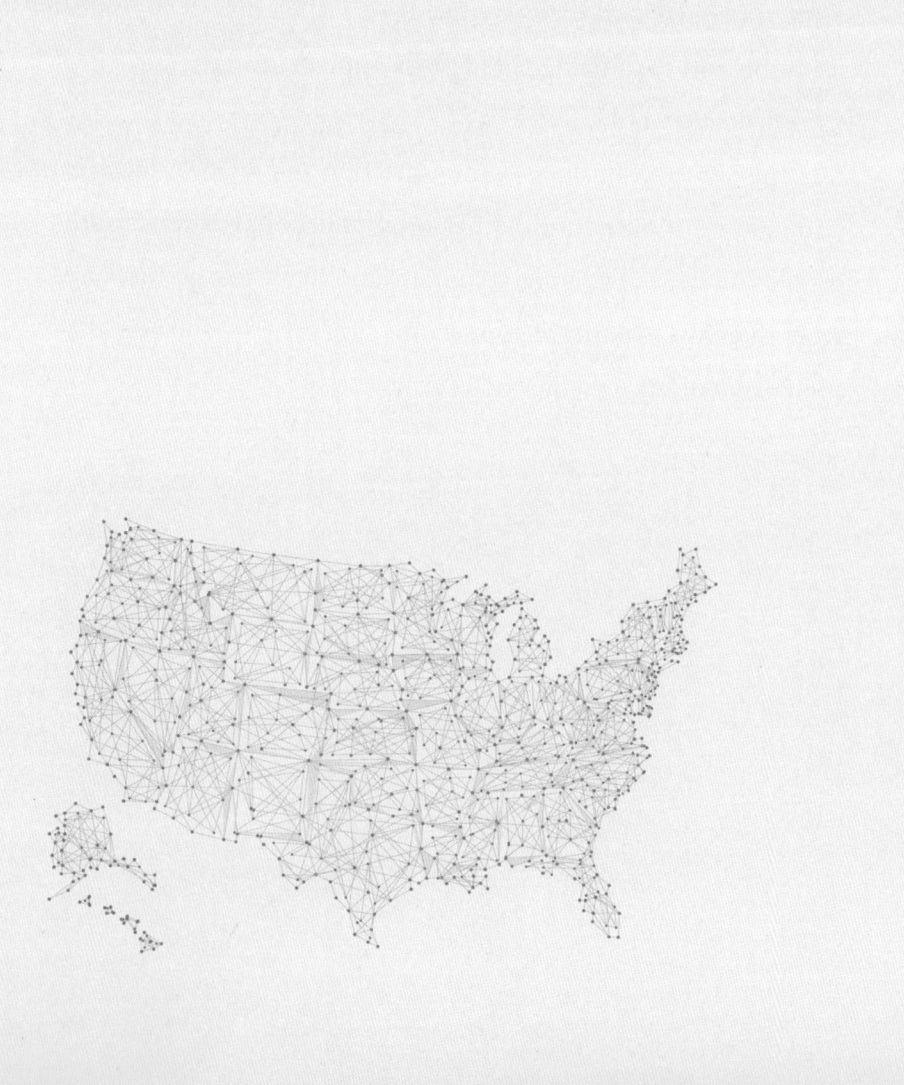

American Business
Understand
Melting Pot and Salad Bowl First

Individualism and Collectivism Coexist

Banana and Onion

There is an analogy often used when comparing the East and West in cultural terms: Westerners are like bananas, and Easterners are like onions. In other words, Westerners are often compared to bananas; once you can peel away their outer layer, their true nature is readily revealed. In contrast, Easterners are likened to onions; even as you peel back layer after layer, their core essence remains elusive and harder to grasp.

Similarly, as mentioned in the Communication and Listening section, the West is a "low context culture," or a culture of direct expression. At the same time, the East is a "high context culture," or a culture of metaphor. Here, the word "context" refers to the atmosphere, background, and nuances involved in communication.

Americans tend to express their thoughts directly through conversation. From a young age, they are encouraged to communicate clearly, which makes them articulate and comfortable speaking in public, regardless of their education or profession.

Americans tend to take conversations literally and express their intentions clear. This direct conversation style might sometimes come across as rude or self-centered to Koreans.

In contrast, Koreans are more likely to use metaphorical expressions and indirect communication. They often rely on facial expressions and gestures to convey their thoughts, expecting the other person to understand the underlying meaning. This approach can sometimes lead to misunderstandings, as the speaker may assume they have been clear, while the listener interprets the message differently.

Many misunderstandings and conflicts between Koreans and Americans arise from differences in values, customs, and manners shaped by their distinct historical cultures. To foster positive relationships between East and West, particularly between Koreans and Americans, and to ensure the smooth operation of a multinational organization, it is essential to understand the differing mindsets that can lead to misunderstandings and conflicts. Recognizing these cultural nuances is the first step toward creating an environment of mutual respect and collaboration. With this in mind, I'd like to share the following insights, which aim to bridge the gap between these distinct perspectives and pave the way for more harmonious and productive interactions.

In South Korea, the collective mindset emphasizes dignity and respect, placing great importance on valuing others' sense of honor. Harmony is pursued to maintain amicable relationships, often agreeing to disagree prioritizing "agreeing to disagree" to avoid conflict. In contrast, the American individualistic mindset centers on the individual as the fundamental unit of society, valuing uniqueness and independence. Mutual competition is seen as a driver for growth and achievement. This contrast underscores a key difference: Koreans are primarily relationship- and process-oriented, while Americans are more action- and results-oriented. Understanding these distinct approaches can help bridge cultural gaps and foster better collaboration between the two perspectives.

Koreans prefer others to recognize and acknowledge their

Banana and Onion.

achievements rather than claiming credit themselves. In contrast, Americans are more proactive in self-promotion and view it as natural. Even if their accomplishments seem minor from a Korean perspective, Americans openly promote them, often receiving immediate recognition or reward, whether tangible or intangible. Positive contributions are quickly rewarded, while poor performance is met with immediate caution, warnings, or even dismissal.

Of course, there are some side effects to these cultural approaches. Emotionally, Americans may experience feelings of isolation or loneliness despite their focus on individuality and independence, potentially undermining their self-esteem and fulfillment. Koreans, on the other hand, might invest significant time and effort in tasks that are unnecessary or unproductive, driven by the collective desire for belonging and security.

Americans tend to focus more on "what" of their actions rather than the "how" or "why," and are less concerned with how others perceive them. They are likely to express their opinions clearly and, even in disagreement, strive to resolve issues through reasoned debate. Once a decision is made, they accept it and generally avoid complaining behind others' backs.

High schools in the United States have "debating clubs." It is an extracurricular activity that encourages young people to

> The West is a "low context culture," a culture of direct expression. And the East is a "high context culture," a culture of metaphor.

debate, discuss, and argue to express themselves clearly and persuasively and to instill rational thinking. The focus here is on expressing one's thoughts and feelings honestly and directly to their counterparts in a debate. Vague expressions are not appreciated by Americans, and Koreans may perceive this directness as disrespectful or cold. Conversely, Americans often interpret vagueness or avoidance of confrontation as signs of insecurity or incompetence.

Americans deeply value the principle that choices, decisions, and actions are personal freedoms, as long as they do not harm others. They take direct offense when these freedoms are infringed upon. Working overtime is similarly viewed as an individual right or choice, whether voluntary or requested. If this right is restricted or interfered with, even legal action could be seen as a natural response.

In U.S. society, everyone is considered equal under the law, which ensures equal opportunities and relationships regardless of age, gender, race, position. In contrast, Korean society is influenced by class perceptions tied to occupation, position, age, and wealth, which significantly impact an individual's work and life. This is despite the widely acknowledged belief in Korea that all human beings are inherently equal.

American individualism emphasizes the "me," while Korean collectivism centers on the "we." As a result, Americans tend to be cautious about sharing information, even in the workplace, only disclosing it those who need to know. If information needs to be shared, permission from the owner must be obtained, and extra care should be taken to protect the identity of others. While South Korea now avoids disclosing personal identities, its collectivist roots sometimes lead to the leakage of personal or relevant information, whether publicly or privately. Koreans working in U.S. organizations should be mindful of this cultural difference.

The differences between Korean and American cultures are vast. For Korean-American companies operating in the U.S., where East and West coexist, it is crucial to understand not just the language and manners but also the underlying mindset and values. Only by investing time and effort in understanding each other's cultural backgrounds can fair judgments and decisions about the organization and coworkers be made.

Cultural Generalization Boundaries

Does poor English proficiency reflect
a lack of other skills?

Culture can be defined as the material and spiritual achievements shaped by the behaviors and lifestyles that members of society acquire, share, and pass down to fulfill a specific purpose or ideal of life. However, my personal interpretation is that culture encompasses all the values and methods necessary to live comfortably and conveniently within a given time, place, and community.

Culture develops its unique character as individual tendencies and values extend into families, regions, and nations. These established cultures evolve over generations and are shaped by the era in which they arise. For example, while Millennials, Gen Z, and Baby Boomers may coexist, the overlap in their shared cultural experiences is often limited.

While human nature and instincts are largely consistent across races, national and era-specific cultures are influenced by historical, religious, and social differences. These cultural traits are passed down from one generation to the next.

Tangible cultures, such as food, language, appearance, clothing, and art, are easy to identify. However, intangible cultures, such as traditions, norms, values, ways of thinking, and ethics, are not easy to grasp unless you have experienced them for a long time. Intangible cultures are manifested in the form of thoughts, beliefs, and emotions. Furthermore, historical, religious, and geographical factors significantly shape cultures, and fully understanding them often requires firsthand observation, communication, and experience. Many intangible aspects of culture serve as underlying causes of ethnic and

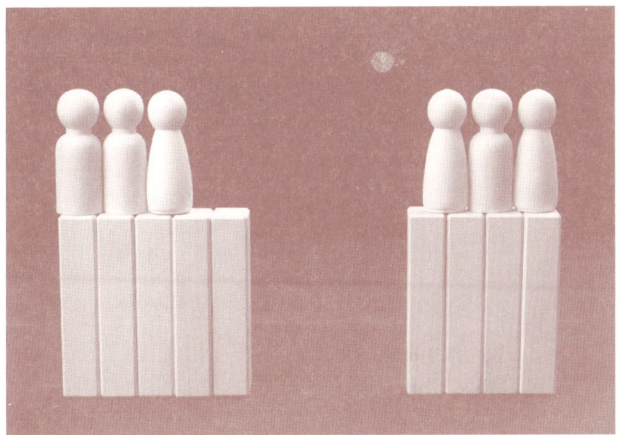

Cultural Misunderstanding and Polarization.

national conflicts.

The complexity, nuance, and subjectivity of culture lie at the heart of these issues, making it crucial to avoid assumptions about other cultures.

In a Korean-American company operating in the United States, both Korean and American cultures coexist, with employees working together toward shared goals. Within this framework, employees collaborate and communicate to deliver high-quality products and services to customers, aiming for optimal outcomes. This practice is fundamental to the success of any company.

However, many challenges arise between members of different cultures that are difficult pinpoint. For example, Americans may mistakenly associate a Korean's limited English proficiency with a lack of other abilities. Similarly, if a Korean doesn't adhere to certain etiquette norms, it might lead to a generalized perception that they come from a less civilized country. These challenges, though rooted in cultural differences, are relatively easier to address since they involve tangible aspects of culture. Enhancing English proficiency and learning American-style etiquette can go a long way in overcoming such misunderstandings.

On the other hand, intangible cultural differences demand greater attention. Traditions, norms, and values from other

> "
> The traditions, norms, and values of other cultures
> are difficult to understand linguistically,
> so it is important to recognize and respect
> the diverse backgrounds behind those traditions, norms, and values.
> "

cultures cannot be fully understood through language alone. It's essential to recognize and respect the diverse backgrounds that shapes these elements. Often, we view our own culture through positive lens, making it challenging to embrace others. This can lead to subjective criticism, defensiveness, or judgment of other cultures—a tendency known as "cultural generalizations."

When cultural generalizations are prevalent in a multiracial organization, they can lead to misunderstandings, accusations, and conflicts between groups, eventually resulting in cultural polarization that hinders productivity.

A lack of respect and trust among employees stemming from culture differences hinders communication and collaboration, fostering a negative workplace atmosphere. Additionally, inconsistent management of tasks and assignments can further diminish productivity. This situation often compels management and human resources to implement inefficient rules and systems to address the challenges of accommodating multiple cultures simultaneously.

Because this issue is often invisible, it is essential to emphasize education, communication, and fostering a positive organizational culture. Individuals should be discouraged from criticizing or condemning other cultures based on subjective judgments. Instead, organizations must create an environment of mutual respect and understanding. Above all, companies should embrace the diverse cultures within their workforce and collaborate with employees to develop a new, shared culture unique to the organization.

A Gap Between
Formal and Pragmatic Logic

Dignity or Saving Face

In Korea, there is a proverb: "Drink cold water and pick my teeth." This reflects the importance Koreans place on maintaining face. For Koreans, maintaining face is tied to pride, politeness, and it plays a significant role in their social interactions.

Based on my knowledge and experience, saving face can be understood as a psychological trait, defined as "the desire to maintain a sense of dignity and avoid shame in one's position, status, wealth, and other aspects of social life and human relationships." From this perspective, the need for self-confidence often leans more toward being other-centered rather than self-centered, focusing on "How do others perceive me?" rather than "Who am I?" In social settings, individuals tend to engage in self-analysis and evaluation based on factors such as appearance, status, wealth, knowledge, happiness.

This tendency is especially strong in groups that are Confucian-minded or who identify as socially upper-class. Even when they are not legally, ethically, or morally wrong, they may feel insulted or embarrassed if they perceive that their dignity has been compromised, based on their subjective and emotional standards.

Saving face manifests in various ways, including bravado, pretense, patience, silence, complicity, and even lying, depending on one's position and circumstances. For example, hosting an extravagant wedding for a child or contributing a large sum of money to a celebration, even if it stretches financial limits, may serve to honor the child and uplifting others. However, these actions are closely tied to maintaining one's own and the family's prestige.

Forcing yourself to conform to your own expectations and goals, despite a disconnect between your material or intellectual capabilities and reality, can manifest as a negative form of pretense. This behavior temporarily bridges the gap between reality and ideals, providing a fleeting sense of mental comfort.

Whenever I visit South Korea, I often observe something peculiar: a noticeable uniformity among people in city centers. From their clothes and hairstyles to their overall appearance, many seem strikingly similar. In the name of fashion, they wear name-brand clothes, bags, and shoes, with features—nose, eyes,

Saving face.

lips—that sometimes make them resemble Barbie dolls. I have often found myself puzzled by youthful faces that seem at odds with their actual age. What began as a trend among a specific demographic of women has now expanded, with cosmetic makeovers becoming increasingly common among men and women of all ages.

I once had the opportunity to go hiking with some friends in South Korea. It was not a very high mountain, and not very rugged. The entire hike was expected to take about three hours, so I put on my trekking shoes, a light running jacket and pants, and headed to the meeting point. When I arrived, I noticed that everyone else was dressed almost identically. Among the dozen of us, we all wore similar hiking attire: boots, hats, sunglasses, and jackets—only the colors varied. An acquaintance looked at me with a puzzled, slightly dismissive expression and asked "Are you going to the mountain dressed like that?" Initially, I was confused by the remark. However, as we climbed, I began to understand. The trail was packed with hikers, young and old, all dressed in remarkably similar outfits. It was a vivid confirmation of what I had heard about Korea: when something becomes popular, it quickly turns into a nationwide trend.

This phenomenon reminds me of the concept of saving face. In a prestige-driven culture that places greater emphasis on outward appearances and formality than on inner values, there is often a strong desire to belong to a particular group, accompanied by a competitive drive for acceptance.

This behavior extends to aspects of Korean society. For instance, during hearings or public discussions, it is common for participants to respond emotionally when the argument does not favor them, rather than addressing the issue with logic and objectivity. This reaction is also rooted in the idea of saving face. Emotional responses often prompt the opposing party to temper their statements out of respect for the other person's dignity. This dynamic creates a cycle in which emotional reactions become the default response to challenging or unfavorable situations.

Saving face has both positive and negative aspects. On the positive side, it promotes politeness, respect, and understanding, which can strengthen relationship and social harmony. However, it can also result in unreasonableness, absurdity, and inefficiency, hindering productivity and objective decision-making.

In contrast, for Americans, the concept of saving face does not hold the same the cultural significance. The phrase is often associated with maintaining appearances or focusing on outward and superficial aspects, and it is generally viewed in a negative light.

Americans tend to be self-centered and pragmatic. They wear thick coats in summer if they're cold and sleeveless clothes in winter if they're hot, without worrying about what others might think of them.

This behavior of Americans may be seen as inappropriate from a Confucian perspective. However, Americans believe that honest expression of one's thoughts and feelings is far more important than pretense. Americans tend to be pragmatic and often struggle to understand the formal logic or subtleties of Korean communication. To Americans, pretense is seen as a distortion of truth, and if something is not what it appears to be, they may regard it as dishonest.

This difference is also reflected in organizational life. For instance, in meetings, the focus is more on discussing the "what" rather than the "how," with clear self-expression and an openness to showing emotions. Americans prioritize their own beliefs and

> Reducing misunderstandings across cultures, countries, and races requires respect, patience, and human consideration. It also demands ongoing exposure to and education about different cultural perspectives.

subjectivity over worrying about others' opinions. As a result, when they believe they are right, they are more likely to stand up for themselves confidently. Even if arguments become heated, Americans tend to accept the final decision and avoid discussing it behind others' backs. Since workplace issues are typically addressed directly and thoroughly, it is uncommon for conflicts to result in lasting rifts between colleagues.

When discussing the concept of saving face, the term "tact (눈치: nunchi)" often comes to mind as a complementary idea. Tact is also centered on others rather than oneself. However, when taken to an extreme, it can lead to defensiveness, distortion, manipulation, dishonesty, and unethical behavior.

However, tact is not always negative. In Korean culture, the concept of "tact (눈치)" is closely tied to the five senses, allowing individuals to observe people, groups, and surrounding atmosphere. Koreans often rely on this heightened awareness to make quick judgments about how other might feel or think. It acts like a radar, enable them to sense the emotions and dynamics around them, allowing for appropriate and timely responses.

Americans tend to be straightforward and matter-of-fact, which can make it challenging for them to fully understand Korean concepts of politeness, dignity, and courtesy. In Korean companies based in the United States, it is not uncommon for these cultural differences to clash. Misunderstandings between the emotional nuances of Korean politeness, moderation, dignity, and sensitivity and the more factual, rational approach common in the U.S., can lead not only to personal conflicts but also to a demeaning perception of the other culture.

This is why it is crucial for Korean-American companies in the U.S. to develop a deep understanding of each other's cultures. Making negative generalizations based on isolated cultural differences, without objective observation and analysis, is both risky and counterproductive. Reducing misunderstandings across cultures, countries, and races requires respect, patience, and genuine human consideration. Additionally, it demands continuous exposure to and education about different cultural perspectives.

Sharing the Korean Sentiment

Shame over guilt, and emotional bond

In the past, I ran an educational consulting firm where I conducted numerous multicultural trainings and workshops for American expatriates and their families. These sessions focused on Korean and Asian cultures, history, values, and business concepts and sentiments, as well as strategies for navigating Korean culture in business and organizational contexts.

At the time, some Korean words and sentiments were particularly challenging to convey to Americans. Classic examples including saving face, tact, shame, and emotional bond (정: Jung). While we have already discussed saving face and tact, today we'll focus on explaining the concepts of shame and emotional bond to Americans.

American cultural experts often use the terms "guilt" and "shame" to highlight the pragmatic tendencies of the West and the formalistic inclinations of the East. While individual values and characteristics naturally vary, it is generally observed that the Western cultures prioritize guilt over shame, whereas Eastern tends to place greater importance on shame than guilt.

Guilt can be defined as "the distressing and uncomfortable feeling experienced when one realizes and acknowledges a wrongdoing or sin they have committed." In essence, it is a psychological response to the awareness that one's actions have violated laws, regulations, or social norms. Typically, when such violations occur, individuals are held accountable through imprisonment, fines, or censure. Once the consequences are faced, guilt often subsides leading to the sentiment, "I have paid my dues!"

In the U.S., where pragmatism dominates, there is a belief that as long as one complies with laws, regulations, social norms, your thoughts, words, and actions should be respected and left unchallenged.

In contrast, shame can be defined as the sense of harm to one's conscience and dignity resulting from a failure to fulfill a responsibility or duty. This concept resonates more deeply with Koreans, who often take a more formalistic approach to social and personal conduct.

Koreans are generally collectivistic, striving to adhere to the group's goals, rules, and values to maintain harmony and a sense of belonging. However, they often experience significant pressure when failing to participate in group activities, whether through non-participation, silence, or avoidance. While such situations typically do not involve legal wrongdoing or harm—thus sparing individuals from feelings of guilt—a strong sense of embarrassment and shame often arises. This shame does not stem from questions of right or wrong but from the avoidance of one's perceived duties and responsibilities.

Next, I would like to explore the concept of emotional bond (情), which I believe is a uniquely Korean emotion that sets Koreans apart from Americans.

In the Korean dictionary, "emotional bond (정)" is defined as

Guilt and Shame.

"the thoughts and feelings that arise from a deep connection to a particular object." Its Chinese character composition includes "heart (心)" and "azure (靑)" symbolizing "a pure and clean heart." While it might be loosely translated into English as "love and hate," this translation fails to capture its full depth and nuance. Numerous expressions in Korea culture are rooted in this profound emotional bond, reflecting its pervasive influence.

Words like "warm," "friendly," "through thick and thin," and even "getting the ick" are deeply embedded in Korean life. For Koreans, warmth evokes feelings of coziness, happiness, family, connection, and home—always carrying a positive connotation.

However, despite its familiarity, explaining the concept of "emotional bond (정)" can be challenging. When asked, "What is emotional bond and affection?" It becomes difficult to articulate through a logical, analytical, or rational perspective, making it even harder to convey to foreigners, including Americans. Emotional bond is a uniquely paradoxical emotion where hate and love coexist, and relationships oscillate between closeness and separation. Through this bond, Koreans can understand unspoken words, communicate through silence, and build deep empathy. This phenomenon is not limited to Korean movies and dramas but is an integral part of everyday life.

Throughout history, Korean concept of emotional bond has

> "
> Each culture is different in its content, methods, and context and cannot be characterized as right or wrong, good or bad.
> "

been the cornerstone of community relationships in Korea's agrarian society. Within this framework, Koreans exchanged traditions and customs, fostering a sense of security, comfort, and warmth. This emotional bond helped to create close-knit in-groups, transcending blood ties or geographical distances. Even in the face of conflicts or animosity, Korean emotional bond remains a powerful emotion, enabling reconciliation and mutual understanding.

However, while emotional bond fosters cohesion, it can also lead to the exclusion of out-groups. Historically, Korea's monolithic cultural identity has made it resistant to foreign influences. Even within the country, strong provincial identities have often caused divisions, with people siding with their region, sometimes regardless of right or wrong.

As demonstrated through the concepts of Korean shame and emotional bond, every culture has its own unique content, methods, and background. These differences should not be judged as right or wrong, good or bad. Instead, it is crucial to embrace diversity in culture, race, language, and values to foster better organizations and promote global harmony. Achieving this requires time, effort, and patience, emphasizing understanding and respecting other cultures rather than clinging solely to our own.

Stereotypes and Misconceptions About the United States

Understand Melting Pot and Salad Bowl first

I remember dining at a Korean restaurant in the United States and sitting next to four middle-aged men. They were all wearing name-brand T-shirts, their collars turned up, and they had golf ball markers in their hats. They looked like they had just finished a round of golf and had come in to eat. I found myself unintentionally listening in on their conversation because of the volume of their voices. They were discussing the political and social realities of the United States and making quick judgments about the country. From their conversation, it was clear that they had not lived in the U.S. for very long.

I learned about a book written by a Korean visitor that was featured in the culture section of a Korean newspaper. The book presented a rather negative account of the author's experience after living in the U.S. for about a year. This made me wonder, "Can someone fully grasp the essence of United States in just

Melting Pot and Salad Bowl.

a year?" and "Is it fair to pass judgment on an entire country based on such a brief stay?" Of course, even for those who live in a place for an extended period, truly understanding its culture requires relevant experience, knowledge, information, and genuine interest. Without these elements, gaining an accurate perspective can remain a challenge.

In a similar vein, I recall my time training Korean expatriates and their families on American culture, relocation, and acculturation. Interestingly, the least effective trainees were not those entirely unfamiliar with the United States but rather those who had spent only a brief time there or felt entitled to judge the country based on second-hand experiences. A lack knowledge can be addressed through learning, but judgments formed from superficial encounters and second-hand information often solidify into prejudices.

The United States is a vast country. Most individuals live within a limited geographic area and time frame, with constrained experience and knowledge. Yet, some confidently assert, "This is what America is." When such voices belong to those with high social status and economic power, their distorted views risk shaping an incomplete or misleading picture of the country.

Immigrants, expatriates, and travelers in the U.S. often experience distinct phases when encountering or adapting to a new culture.

The first is the so-called "tourist phase" or "honeymoon phase," which lasts typically lasts first three to six months. During this period, excitement and curiosity dominates as individuals focus on learning and understanding the new culture. Psychological conflicts are rare, as Americans generally display inclusiveness and hospitality toward short-term visitors and new arrivals.

The second phase is the "confusion and frustration stage," which usually emerges within the first year. By this time, the initial excitement of the move or visit has worn off. As individuals integrate into daily life among Americans, they are no longer seen as visitors but are treated as equals. This shift often brings new challenges and cultural confrontations as they navigate the realities of adapting to a different way of life. This

"
When describing American culture metaphorically, the phrases "melting pot" and "salad bowl" are often used to symbolize "unity" and "uniqueness," respectively.
"

confusion and frustration may lead to feelings of resentment, dislike, or even inferiority toward the U.S. It is not uncommon for individuals to criticize Americans as a way to expressing their negative emotions.

The third stage, known as the "adaptation stage," follows the "confusion and frustration" phase. During this stage, individuals begin to recognize the gap between their expectations and reality and make conscious efforts to bridge it. Over time, you may find themselves gradually embracing the new culture, often without even realizing it. Actively working to understand cultural differences through careful observation and analysis is crucial during this stage, as if helps foster greater acceptance and integration.

For a culture to take shape, Certain basic elements are required, often referred to as the 3Ps: place, people, and period.

First, culture is shaped by geographic regions. For instance, the New England area in the Northeastern U.S. is generally conservative, while the West Coast, especially California, is known for its liberal values. The "Bible belt" in the South is heavily influenced by religion and regional pride. These regional differences result in distinct cultural variations, even within the U.S.

Next, culture is shaped by specific people, or demographics. Populations are often categorized by income levels—high, middle, or low—and by occupation, with white-collar workers referring to professionals and mental labors, and blue-collar to those in manual labors. Additionally, the U.S. comprises a diverse range of racial and ethnic groups, including white, black, Latino, and Asian populations. This mix of demographics and social classes creates unique and sometimes surprising cultural dynamics.

In addition, specific generations and time periods play a pivotal role in shaping culture. Older generations often have distinct mindsets and lifestyles compared to younger ones, and as times progresses, culture naturally evolves. The culture of 1000 years ago is vastly different from that of 100 years ago, just as today's culture will differ from that of 100 years in the future.

When describing American culture, metaphors like the "melting pot" and the "salad bowl" are often invoked. The "melting pot" symbolizes unity through blending, while the "salad bowl" highlights the preservation of individual identities within a collective whole.

The United States has a rich history shaped by immigration, evolving into a federation where diverse races from around the world come together as equal members in pursuit of common goals.

The "melting pot" metaphor symbolizes the unity of different races and cultures blending together to achieve shared objectives within the "crockpot" of America. In contrast, the "salad bowl" represents the diversity of races and cultures in the U.S., where each retain its unique characteristics, flavors, and colors, much like the vegetables and fruits in a bowl.

Recognizing this, Koreans in the U.S. should strive to maintain pride in their heritage and roots while actively contributing to the growth and prosperity of the U.S. and its communities as Americans or residents or citizens. This calls for a positive and proactive approach, one that seeks to understand and appreciate American culture rather than criticizing it. By living alongside Americans and embracing their perspectives, words, and behaviors, Koreans can foster meaningful communication and connections, ultimately serving as civilian diplomat for Korea and engaged citizens of the United States.

The Difference Between Friendliness and Friendship

I do not know about you

Americans are generally friendly, often smiling and Americans are generally friendly, often smiling and greeting strangers in passing. In contrast, Koreans may appear more reserved or expressionless when interacting with unfamiliar people. This difference may stem from the range of concerns Koreans face throughout their lives, including intense competition for school admissions, building resumes, securing jobs, purchasing homes (mainly apartments in Korea), educating their children, and planning for retirement. These challenges are often viewed as personal, family, and social missions that must be accomplished, contributing to a more serious demeanor.

As a new immigrant or expatriate beginning life in the United States, obtaining the right information is crucial for quickly settling yourself and your family. Before the widespread use of the internet and smartphones, much of this information had to be gathered through personal experience or by asking others. For those not fluent in English, this often resulted in inconvenience, embarrassment, and at times, scorn. While many aspects of American culture might seem like common sense to Americans, they can come as a shock to Koreans. The most effective way to navigate these challenges was to seek guidance from experienced and knowledgeable immigrants or expatriates who had already established themselves in the U.S.

I recall an anecdote about a Korean-American couple who had recently settled in the United States. The husband, an intermediate English speaker with no local connections, struggled with the challenges of daily life. Fortunately, one of his American coworkers kindly answered his many questions about life in the U.S. and share practical advice based on personal experiences. Over time, the husband began to view this coworker as a close and reliable friend.

Cultural learning process.

About a month later, the Korean couple decided to show their gratitude by hosting a Korean dinner at their home. They planned a traditional meal, including bulgogi, and extended an invitation to the coworker and his wife. The husband, deeply appreciative of his coworker's help, eagerly looked forward to the evening. However, the American coworker politely declined the invitation, explaining that he already had a prior commitment.

A few days later, still eager to show his appreciation, the husband asked again, inquiring about the coworker's availability for a couple's dinner. This time, the American coworker politely responded, "I don't know you well yet, and my wife isn't fond of Asian food. I appreciate the invitation, but I will have to decline." To the husband's surprise, what he had perceived as a building friendship was simply an act of kindness on the part of the American coworker.

This experience highlights the difference between friendliness and friendship. In Korea, when people share mutual liking and common values, they often form friendships based on trust and loyalty. These bond can deepen further when there are shared factors such as age, background, or experiences. In contrast, while Americans are generally friendly, they do not as readily form deep, personal friendships, often reserving those connections for relationships that develop over time and shared experiences.

These cultural differences in attitudes toward kindness and friendship largely stem from the historical and social backgrounds of each country. The United States, for instance, has a history shaped by settlement and migration. First, the Puritans crossed the Atlantic with dreams of building a new world. After establishing themselves in the east, they faced struggles against Native Americans and the harshness of nature as they pursued wealth and prosperity. This relentless pursuit continued westward, driving the expansion across the continent. The United States spans over 3,000 miles from east to west and approximately 1,500 miles from north to south, making life in New York on the east coast and California on the west coast feel like entirely different nations.

I discovered that the average American relocates across the country or state lines roughly once every five years for reasons such as family, education, or work. This mobility has shaped in the U.S. into a highly dynamic society. With each move, Americans frequently form new relationships in unfamiliar environments. To navigate these transitions, they rely on building positive connections, where kindness plays a crucial role in fostering and maintaining these relationships.

As a result, Americans have grown accustomed to forming

> Differences in historical and social backgrounds lead to cultural differences, which in turn manifest in language and expression. For example, the American word for "kindness" and the Korean word for "friendship."

and ending relationships frequently. This pattern is shaped by historical trends and the modern social and professional demands frequent relocation. In this context, kindness serves as a practical and less burdensome alternative to deep friendships, making it more suitable for everyday interactions.

On the other hand, many Asian countries, including Korea, have historically been agrarian societies. Generations of farmers lived and worked in the same communities, fostering strong relationships and mutual support to assist neighbors during harvests.

These cultures thrived on a sense of belonging and solidarity.

However, Korea is currently experiencing significant westernization, with individualism gaining ground, particularly among younger generations. As a result, Koreans may now choose to prioritize kindness or adopt new ways of life in response to these shifting culture dynamics.

Differences in historical and social backgrounds give rise to cultural differences, which are often reflected in language and expression. Previously, we described Korean and American communication styles as "high context" and "low context," respectively. In this context, "high" and "low" refers to the degree of reliance on implicit non-verbal cues for communication. "context" encompasses elements such as facial expressions, gestures, tones, and mood, which shape the overall approach required for effective communication.

To summarize, Korean "high context" communication is rhetorical, qualitative, metaphor-oriented, and comprehensive, while American "low context" communication is straightforward, quantitative, fact-oriented, and linear. "High context" communication relies on multiple layers and subtle cues, whereas "low context" communication takes a more direct and explicit approach.

Metaphors and symbols play a significant role in Korean expression. Rather than starting facts or content directly, Koreans often consider the situation and relationships involved, opting for more indirect language. Facial expressions and tone of voice are also key tools for conveying messages holistically. In this way, Korean "high context" communication integrates a wide range of elements, such as timing, background, environment, and subtle cues like awareness and intuition.

In contrast, Americans tend to be more straightforward in their communication. They present facts and content directly, and when they hear something, they often interpret and understand it in a one-dimensional way. This "low context" approach enables Americans to process words and sentences in a linear and unfiltered manner.

These distinct historical and social backgrounds profoundly influence each country's culture, resulting in notable differences. This dynamic is also evident in the contrast between American "friendliness" and Korean "friendship."

We often believe that our own culture and way of life are the most comfortable and correct. When we encounter unfamiliar situations, it's natural to feel nervous, overwhelmed, or hesitant to embrace them. To overcome this, we must acknowledge our differences and respect the cultures shaped by the other person's region, environment, and era. Immigrants, especially those who have voluntarily entered a cultural melting pot, should strive to be as respectful and accepting of the native culture as possible.

Inherent Characteristics of United States Organizations

"We" or "I"

People who have lived for generations within a particular race, ethnicity or specific region absorb their culture as naturally as they breathe air. For example, when a native of Seoul walks through the familiar streets of Myeong-dong, the sights, sounds, smells, and humidity evoke a sense of comfort and familiarity. However, for a foreigner, the same experience can feel entirely different, even overwhelming. Walking down a street in Korea, the unfamiliar sights and smells can evoke tension and anxiety for those unaccustomed to the environment. Gaining an understanding of Korean culture or having prior experience with it can significantly ease this discomfort. Similarly, Koreans working in American society and organizations can adapt more smoothly if they are aware of cultural differences in advance.

Until the early 2000s, Korea and the U.S. managed their companies and organizations with distinct approach. For instance, large Korean companies often relied on large-scale open recruitment, organizing their workforce around generalist and departmental structures. The goal was to create a collective competitive advantage through the harmony of employees with similar capabilities and mindsets, rather than creating a competitive organizational environment. As a result, new employees often lacked professional qualifications at the outset and were expected to gradually build expertise through education, on-the-job training, and experience. Korean managers typically occupied a space between "specialists" and "generalists": they could handle a variety of roles but often lacked deep expertise in specific functions. Additionally, the system for job evaluation, promotion, and compensation was largely based on collective and uniform factors, such as date of hire and seniority, although individual ability and performance were also considered important.

Recently, however, organizations in Korea have been shifting from open recruitment to rolling recruitment, similar to practices in the United States. With a declining birthrate, an aging population, the changing lifestyles of Millennials and Gen Z, and the need for globalization to maintain a competitive advantage, the traditional Japanese approach to a job is fading in Korea, giving way to an American-style meritocracy.

In the U.S., organizations typically hire to meet immediate needs and circumstances, seeking candidates with the requisite skills, experience, education, and attitude for specific roles. Even for recent graduates, U.S. employers prioritize a broad range of experiences. Internships and related activities during college often serve as key indicators of a candidate's level of competence and preparedness.

In American organizations, long-term employment is virtually non-existent, and promotions based solely on seniority are extremely rare. It is a culture where you can ask for a promotion or reward if you meet performance expectations, but you can also be terminated at any time without notice if you do not meet them. As a result, employees in the U.S. are not constantly under the watchful eye of their supervisor. Instead, the focus is on results and performance rather than the sheer amount of work done or hours spent. This approach encourages individuals to remain competitive in the job market. Employees view themselves as valuable assets, frequently updating their skills and career paths to maximize their compensation and opportunities. This dynamic fosters a significant amount of invisible competition, not only within teams but also among employees performing similar tasks. Consequently, job evaluations in American companies tend to be quantitative, objective, and short-term. Unlike Korean companies, which traditionally assess employees based on loyalty, dedication, and sacrifice to the organization or supervisor, American companies evaluate employees by analyzing the labor market value of a specific role. They compare job responsibilities, performance, and salary level using supply-and-demand principles, determining an employee's value based on objective and relative criteria.

In U.S. organizations, roles take precedence over titles, with R&R referring to roles and responsibilities clearly outlined in job descriptions. The duties, authority, and accountability associated with each position are typically well-defined, and the decision-making process is concise and straightforward. Employees are granted the authority and budget necessary to fulfill their tasks, and their performance is evaluated objectively and fairly, which informs decisions on compensation, promotion, or termination. However, U.S. management is highly sensitive to short-term business results and performance metrics, making personnel decisions, particularly those related to rewards, both swift and decisive. Companies in the U.S do not hesitate to terminate employees for poor performance or failed assignments, which creates a competitive organizational culture driven by results and performance.

These characteristics differ significantly from Korean

organizations, which tend to operate in more close-knit environments. As a result, companies with both American and Korean employees require a management approach that embraces cultural diversity. Prioritizing an understanding of employees' values and mindsets, along with implementing training programs that promote mutual respect, is essential.

Recognizing cultural differences is fundamental to fostering effective communication and collaboration, as it involves understanding individuals beyond mere language. With this in mind, let's delve into some key cultural differences in organizations where Americans and Koreans work together.

First, consider the concept of time.

Historically, Korea was an agrarian society where people

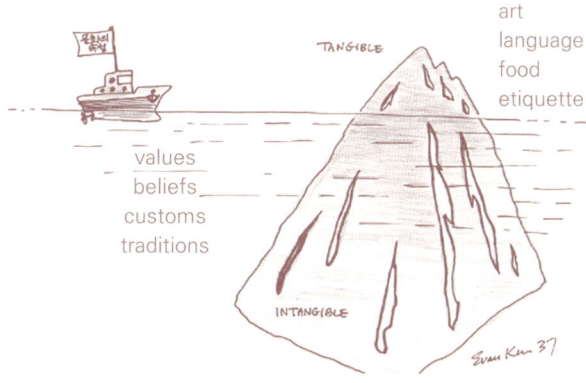

Cultural differences.

settled in specific areas and lived in tune with nature. The rhythm of life was governed by natural cycles—seasons, weather, and the characteristics of crops—allowing people to align their activities with nature's timing. As a result, the Korean concept of time can be described as "flowing." Rather than managing, controlling, or optimizing time, Koreans traditionally aimed to live in harmony with it. Additionally, this long-term communal lifestyle fostered close kinship relationships among family and relatives, instilling values such as harmony, unity, patience, and obedience, all within a system of manners and norms.

In contrast, the concept of time in the United States evolved from its history as a frontier society. Early settlers frequently moved from east to west, driven by the need for survival and the pursuit of new opportunities. They established temporary bases by pitching tents in suitable pastures or, for longer stays, constructed log cabins equipped with only the bare necessities. This cycle of migration, pioneering, and adventure emphasized individual effort—"I"—over collective action—"we." Consequently, the American concept of time places a strong emphasis on management, control, and efficiency. This mindset is evident in expressions like "wait for a second," highlighting the value of precision and urgency.

Now, consider the concept of relationships. The agrarian roots of Korea society and the frontier-driven history of the United States fostered two distinct cultural orientations: collectivism in Korea and individualism in the United States. These contrasting foundations have deeply influenced how human relationships are structured and valued in each culture.

Korea's agricultural society required significant labor for tasks like planting and harvesting, so people lived communally with their immediate and extended families, often spanning three or four generations. Cooperation and unity were essential for smooth farming operations, which led to the development of manners and norms, including hierarchical structures. Values such as harmony, loyalty, sacrifice, consideration, patience, adaptability, courtesy, and respect were highly emphasized. Communication became indirect, introverted, and metaphorical, focusing on consideration for others rather than oneself. Those who were negatively stigmatized were often pressured to leave the community.

These cultural characteristics have deeply influenced South Korean organizations. Seniority, determined by age and status, has traditionally been highly valued, with dignity, authority, and saving face considered as important as competence and attitude. Organizational culture emphasized interpersonal harmony and consensus over performance or results. However, this approach has not been without its drawbacks. It has sometimes fostered or tacitly condoned unethical practices and, in recent years, has led to growing intergenerational conflicts. These tensions have been fueled by shifting societal awareness and the influence of Westernization, driven by Korea's economic growth.

The American frontier, in contrast, emphasized the individual as the cornerstone of society. The vast landscapes and the challenges of protecting families fostered a culture driven by independent rights and abilities rather than cooperation or unity. This environment cultivated a strong sense of self-reliance, making Americans more independent, direct, and outspoken. Hierarchical considerations held less sway, allowing individuals to freely express their thoughts and opinions. Additionally, Americans became adept at self-promotion, highlighting even the smallest contributions or achievements as part of their personal narrative.

This cultural mindset makes it challenging for Americans to understand why Koreans often endure inconvenience or dissatisfaction without expressing their true feelings or why they may accept material and psychological losses for the sake of dignity or patience. Americans may interpret this reluctance to speak up as hypocrisy or insincerity, and they often mistake modesty and humility for a lack of confidence or competence.

"
A company with a mix of Americans and Koreans
needs to be culturally sensitive,
understand the values and mindsets of its employees,
and train them on mutual respect as a core value.

"

When exploring American individualism, privacy becomes is a key factor.

In the U.S., there is a long-standing tradition of maintaining respectful distancing, often referred to "personal space" or "bubble space." This space typically ranges from 1.5 to 4 meters (5 to 13 feet), with anything closer considered "intimate space," reserved for lovers or close friends. Americans make a conscious strive to respect this social norm, even in crowded settings. If someone unintentionally invades another person's personal space, Americans usually apologize or ask for permission, as failing to do so is considered impolite.

Similarly, Americans are highly sensitive about personal information. When such details are required, explicit consent is always sought from the individual. Topics like age, weight, marital status, divorce, children, religion, property, and income are handled with caution, and sharing this information with third parties permission consent is strongly avoided. If personal information is inappropriately disclosed, legal action is a common recourse. This cultural norm is something Koreans, who are more accustomed to sharing personal details in a collectivistic society, should keep in mind when navigating American society or organizations.

It is also essential to reflect on the concept of equality (egalitarianism) versus prejudice based on social class (classism). Since President Abraham Lincoln's Emancipation Proclamation in the mid-19th century, the United States has actively pursued equality. The fundamental right has been reinforced by the efforts and sacrifices of figures like Rosa Parks and the Civil Rights Movement led by Dr. Martin Luther King Jr. These efforts have since evolved into robust legal and institutional frameworks. For instance, federal law protects against discrimination based on age, gender, race, national origin, color, physical condition (including disability), religion, creed, and sexual preference. These laws ensure equal opportunities and prohibit discriminatory practices and abuse. Furthermore, legislation such as the Civil Rights Act, labor laws, and affirmative action initiatives continue to promote and uphold equality.

The nature of discrimination in South Korea differs different from that in the United States. As a largely mono-ethnic nation, racism in South Korea does not manifest in the same as it does in the U.S. Instead, classism has historically played a dominant role. Rooted in the traditional status system and shaped by collectivist values, this classism has evolved into a modern dynamic where materialism delineates "lords and peasants." In recent years, South Korea has seen the rise of individuals in politics, the economy, and society who flaunt their status, position, power, and wealth, further emphasizing this new class divide.

Additionally, pragmatism and formalism distinguish the United States from South Korea. Individualism and egalitarianism prevalent in the U.S. naturally foster a pragmatic mindset, while South Korea's collectivism and classism often encourage a more formalistic approach.

For example, Bill Clinton, the 42nd president of the United States, faced impeachment due to a scandal involving a woman but remained in office because public opinion favored his ability to continue performing his presidential duties. In contrast, the older generation in Korea often reacts emotionally rather than rationally, favoring clear, black-and-white judgments over nuanced perspectives. This tendency can sometimes lead to witch-hunt-style accusations.

Americans are generally more inclined toward rationality,

logic, realism, and objectivity, whereas Koreans often prioritize harmony, formality, pretense, and emotion. These cultural tendencies significantly influence organizational dynamics, underscoring the importance understanding differing values when working across cultures.

I would like to highlight other organizational unity events, such as picnics. When working as an expatriate for a large Korean company, we organized a Saturday picnic to welcome the newly appointed head of the U.S. subsidiary and to encourage socialization among employees. The event was designed to include Korean and American employees, expatriates and their families. However, during the planning process, we encountered some unexpected questions: "I cannot make it on a Saturday. Can we reschedule for a weekday?" "How much overtime will be paid for the personal time dedicated to the company?" "Will babysitting services be provided during the event?" Despite these inquires, the picnic proceeded as planned. Interestingly, the American employees arrived late, spent most of their time with their families, and did not offer any apologies for their tardiness.

Americans are meticulous about their work responsibilities, obligations, and fulfilling contracts or promises. They place a high value on their right to use personal time freely, as long as they comply with basic regulations and do not harm others.

When work-related activities encroach on their personal time, they expect appropriate compensation. Additionally, many Americans will take legal action to recover both tangible and intangible losses when they feel their rights or interests have been violated.

In contrast, South Korea's collectivistic society often places more restrictions on individual freedoms, which can make the American approach seem selfish and materialistic. However, it's important to understand that America culture generally emphasize the "I" perspective more than the "we," reflecting a stronger focus on individual rights and autonomy.

Basic Manners
in American Organizations

When in Rome, do as the Romans do

The importance of understanding Korea's traditions, customs, and ideas cannot be overstated when working within American society and organizations.

Approximately 20 to 30 years ago, Korea was not viewed positively in the United States. Limited, subjective, and often negative experiences with certain Americans contributed to generalized and unfavorable stereotypes about the country. However, in recent years, this perception has significantly improved. Korea's rise as one of the world's top 10 economies, the global popularity of its pop culture—such as K-pop and Korean films—and advancements in technologies like semiconductors and the Internet have contributed to its enhanced reputation. Given this shift, international students, expatriates, immigrants, and even travelers to the U.S., need to be mindful of their behavior and attitudes. Representing Korea positively in personal and professional interactions can further strengthen these improved perceptions and foster greater mutual understanding. It is crucial to understand and adhere to the fundamental conventions and etiquette of American society and organizations. While many of these practices may seem like common sense, they are not always easy to implement without full internalization. This process requires continuous attention, effort, and a willingness to adapt.

Handshake

When shaking hands with an American, it is important to maintain eye contact, smile, and give a firm yet moderate handshake, typically shaking it three or four times. Avoid placing your left hand under your right, combining a handshake with a bow, or breaking eye contact, as these gestures are considered inappropriate. Traditionally, women were expected to initiate a handshake with a men, but this custom has largely faded in modern times.

Eye Contact

When speaking to an American, always maintain eye contact, as it conveys respect and a willingness to engage openly and honestly. While Koreans may avoid direct eye contact with someone higher in the hierarchy out of respect—a practice rooted in Confucianism—Americans might interpret this behavior as a sign of insincerity or lack of confidence.

Business Card

Americans do not place as much importance on business cards as Koreans do. While Americans may casually handle or even jot notes on them, some Koreans view business cards as a reflection of personal identity and treat them with great respect.

Conversation

Americans often start conversations with casual topics such as the weather, sports, vacations, hobbies, or current events. To build rapport, it is best to avoid asking certain personal questions unless you have a close relationship.

Financial matters: Avoid questions about income or assets, such as financial situation, primary source of income, or real estate ownership.

Physical characteristics: Steer clear of inquires about age, weight, height, and appearance. While compliments on appearance, particularly for women, are sometimes acceptable, they can be misinterpreted as sexual harassment.

Ideology: Discussions on topics like politics and religion

"Si fueris Romae, Romano vivito more"

When in Rome, do as the Romans do.

should generally be avoided, as these subjects have become increasingly polarizing, especially since Donald Trump's presidency.

Family matters: Avoid asking about marital status or whether they have children unless the individual brings it up. These topics can touch on personal or difficult circumstances that may not be immediately apparent.

It is also important to be mindful of American employees when communicating within Korean companies operating in the U.S. Since a significant proportion of employees are often Koreans, office conversations are often conducted in Korean. This can leave American employees, who may be in the minority, feeling excluded or marginalized. Additionally, they may feel uncomfortable or even offended if their names are mentioned in a language they don't understand. While using Korean when necessary is entirely acceptable, it's considerate to either switch to English or ask for permission before referencing American employees in the conversation. This simple gesture helps foster inclusivity and mutual respect within the workplace.

Appointment and Invitation

In the U.S., it is customary to give at least a week's notice for appointments or invitations. For formal events, such as weddings, an RSVP is expected, and failing to attend after promising to do so without prior notice is considered impolite.

In most service industries, reservations are required and treated as commitments. Canceling late or not at all can cause financial loss to the business owner and is viewed negatively.

Americans place high value on their time and that of others, which is reflected in the emphasis U.S. organizations place on time management and results. Employees who linger in the office waiting for their bosses to leave may be perceived as inefficient or lacking in competence.

Similarly, there is a strong sense of accountability when it comes to meeting work deadlines or providing advance notice if commitments cannot be met. Offering a timely and reasonable

> In America, to ensure positive treatment
> and avoid unnecessary misunderstanding or prejudice,
> it is crucial to understand and adhere to the basic conventions and etiquette
> of American society and organizations.

explanation in such cases is not just polite but expected.

Meal

Americans tend to take longer than Koreans when eating, especially dinner, which can last two hours or more. When dining with Americans, it is helpful to prepare conversational topics or engage in common-sense discussions to maintain the flow of the meal.

If you find it challenging to participate fully in the conversation due to language barriers, consider hosting the meal at a Korean restaurant. This setting provides an opportunity to steer the discussion toward Korean culture, making easier to engage. Alternatively, increasing the number of people at the table can foster a more social atmosphere. A balanced mix of Korean and American diners, with limited use of Korean during the meal, can help create a more inclusive and friendly environment.

It is also important to avoid making gurgling or slurping noises while eating, as these considered impolite in American dining culture. If you have food in your mouth, refrain from speaking and be careful not to show it. Burping at the table is especially frowned upon: if it happens, a polite "Excuse me!" is expected. On the other hand, blowing your nose at the table is generally acceptable in American dining culture.

When it comes to shared dishes, always use the designated serving utensils for taking food from communal plates. Avoid picking up or scooping food directly onto your plate with your own utensils, as this is considered unsanitary.

Physical Touch

In recent years, the United States has witnessed the rise of the "Me Too" movement, as stories of sexual violence against women have been exposed and publicized. Inappropriate behavior, threats, and demands directed at women—often perpetrated by those in positions of power, status, or wealth—have been met with significant consequences. As awareness of these issues has increased, sexually inappropriate behavior, including unwanted touching, has become an especially sensitive topic in

U.S. workplaces. Organizations have responded by intensifying training programs and implementing stronger systems, particularly for senior management.

In the U.S., sexual harassment is broadly defined as "any behavior that makes someone feels uncomfortable." Since this definition is both relative and subjective, it is essential to ensure that all behavior, including physical contact, is respectful and unlikely to offend.

Cultural attributes can be likened to an iceberg. The visible tip above the water represents such as language, rituals, art, traditions, and manners-elements that are easily observed and learned through the senses. However, the larger mass below the surface contains the deeper values, beliefs, and ways of thinking that are fundamental to the culture, which can only be fully understood through years of direct and indirect experience. Mastering even the visible aspects of culture can help establish positive relationships and facilitate effective collaboration, especially with Americans.

To that end, it is worth remembering the saying, "When in Rome, do as the Romans do." In the U.S., respecting their culture and adopting their perspective is important, while also staying active and proud of your own heritage.

Epilogue

Competencies Required for Leading Diverse Organizations in the United States

As I close my laptop on this crisp Saturday morning, having finished the final section of my manuscript, the tension and responsibilities of the writing process seem to melt away, leaving me with a sense of peaceful awareness. Today, the coffee tastes richer, the blossoms on the magnolia tree outside my window, appear brighter, and the bees buzzing around them hold my attention more than usual. Perhaps it is because, for a brief moment, I have let go of my purpose and goals, allowing myself to simply be present, appreciating my surroundings without consciously deciding what to see or hear.

We spend most of our lives within various social and

organizational structures. From our mid-to-late twenties, when formal education typically concludes, until retirement, we belong to groups that shape our daily lives. In these settings, we live, work, and compete in environments influenced by diverse cultures and circumstances—sometimes by choice, other times by necessity—on an uncertain journey toward fulfillment and happiness.

My journey began in 1985 when I became an expatriate working for a new organization in the United States. Initially, I was overly confident in my English proficiency and professional expertise. However, the cultural shocks I encountered led to frustration, misunderstandings, and even personal and professional setbacks. It was a humbling period of trial and error.

Through ongoing reflection, I realized that success in communication and performance required a deep understanding of American culture, its people, and its business practices. Determined to adapt, I dedicated myself to learning, and six years later, I published a book titled "The Guide to Living in America." Revisting those memories and reflecting on nearly four decades of life and work in the U.S., I feel a renewed sense of responsibility and excitement for the journey ahead.

The common goal of for-profit organizations is often summarized as "delivering the best products and services at the most competitive price while, generating the highest profit." However, in global and bicultural organizations with diverse workforces, success relies not only on the technical aspects—products, services, and systems—but also on the cultural mindset and values of the people. Even with the most efficient organizational structures in place, it is ultimately the people who make success possible. Trust, respect, communication, and collaboration are the true drivers of achievement. This book seeks to share insights gained through years of firsthand experience, offering guidance to navigate the complexities of diverse organizations.

A simple definition of culture is "the collection of elements that make daily life comfortable, familiar, and secure." While this includes food, clothing, art, and language, true cultural understanding requires delving deeper into traditions, customs, beliefs, and values. It is a mistake to assume that fluency in English or long-term residence in the U.S. equates to a full understanding of American society, culture, or people.

To successfully manage a for-profit organization in the U.S., leaders need more than the standard training in leadership and collaboration. They must also master the nuances of American culture, values, communication styles, and business practices—critical skills for effectively leading a bicultural organization.

In Korea, there is a saying: There is no place like home. It challenges of adapting to unfamiliar environments. Even within a homogeneous culture, generational and regional differences can complicate organizational dynamics. Managing a multicultural organization in the U.S. requires flexibility, cultural sensitivity, and a multidimensional approach to leadership.

Just as maintaining physical health requires regular cardio and strength training, strong leadership and management skills tangible results requires practice, persistence, and a commitment to growth. Leadership cannot be developed through theoretical learning alone; it is built over time through repeated efforts and the formation of effective habits.

With that in mind, I would like to share key insights from my experience leading bicultural organizations. These insights highlight the essential competencies needed to manage people and organizations in a diverse environments—competencies that, like muscles, require deliberate development and ongoing strengthening.

Linguistic Muscle

Proficiency in English is vital for collaboration, communication, and overall job performance. Without strong English skills, your competence in the workplace may come into question. While fluency in pronunciation and tone is advantageous, at the very least, you should be able to clearly organize your thoughts and communicate them effectively to others.

Intellectual Muscle

As a practitioner, manager, or executive, possessing essential management skills, knowledge, and information is fundamental. However, if you prioritize status, authority, or theoretical critiques over intellectual engagement, the quality of your leadership will inevitably decline. Continuous learning and intellectual growth are crucial, and effectively applying these insights to your role is key to achieving lasting success.

Culture Adaptation Muscle

Adapting to a new culture is a complex, ongoing process. While the initial stages are often marked by excitement and anticipation, challenges and culture shock inevitably follow. Successfully navigating these hurdles is key to understanding, accepting, and adapting to a different culture.

Failing to do so can lead prejudices, misunderstandings, and conflicts rooted in limited experiences. Defensive attitudes, such as assuming "I am right, and they are wrong," can result in harmful generalizations, lower morale, and even racial tensions within diverse organizations.

Relationship Muscle

In bicultural organizations, success largely hinges on the people within them, making the dynamics of communication and attitude crucial.

Effective communication, especially when using a non-native language, requires understanding, responding to, and aligning with the other person's perspective. This concept, often referred to as "eye-level synchronization," involves meeting others where they are in terms of communication. Just as parents adjust their language to match their child's comprehension, professionals must adapt their communication style to effectively engage with individuals from diverse generations, ethnicities, or roles. Additionally, treating others with respect, courtesy, and humility, regardless of their status, fosters meaningful connections. While people in diverse organizations come from varied cultural backgrounds, we all share common instincts and emotions.

Demonstrating authenticity, humility, and consideration helps cultivate deeper relationships and strengthens leadership effectiveness.

We spend a significant portion of our lives interacting with others in organizational settings, contributing to shared goals through collaboration. In these environments, we seek fulfillment, achievement, and happiness, often through perseverance and hard work.

It is my hope that this book offers valuable insights to those navigating diverse, bicultural environments, helping them achieve their personal and professional aspirations. If you have any questions or thoughts, please feel free to email me at "eunsungkim@aol.com" I welcome the opportunity to connect and engage with you.

My knowledge comes from trenches of diverse organizations, earned through hard-fought experience. I encourage you to embrace these challenges as well-this practical, "street-smart" wisdom is something that cannot be fully conveyed through theory alone.

It is my heartfelt hope that you thrive as professionals—whether as expatriates, managers, leaders, executives, entrepreneurs, or family members—within diverse organizations. Moreover, I hope you will serve as civilian diplomats, representing our country with pride and helping to bridge the cultural gap between Korea and the United States.

Evan Eun Sung Kim

Milestones for Global Leaders' Success
in the United States

초판 1쇄 발행 2025년 2월 14일

지은이　　김은성
옮긴이　　최형윤 김은성

펴낸이　　노현덕
펴낸곳　　마오르
브랜드　　MAOWR

편집　　　이재형 최형윤
디자인　　조유영
마케팅　　박서원
경영지원　김남용

등록　　　2023년 5월 10일 제2023-000065호
주소　　　경기도 성남시 분당구 서현로 210번길 1 405호
전화　　　031-8028-0202
팩스　　　0504-482-9315
이메일　　business@maowr.com
홈페이지　www.maowr.com

ISBN 979-11-983891-3-8(03320)

* 이 책은 저작권법에 의해 보호받는 저작물이므로 무단 전재와 복제를 금하며,
  이 책의 내용 전부 또는 일부를 이용하려면 반드시 저작권자와 마오르 주식회사의 서면 동의를 받아야 합니다.

* 파본은 구입처에서 교환해 드립니다.

* 가격은 뒤표지에 표시돼 있습니다.